PRAISE FOR *BEHIND THE SHATTERED CHURCH*

The reverend Dr. Willis Lawton gives us a scholarly review of church history with objective accuracy. Terrible divisions have happened, many times out of arrogance, pride, and impatience. Dr. Lawton appeals to the body of Christ to put priority on the words of Jesus in his high priestly prayer from John 17, that "they may all be one; even as You, Father, are in Me and I in You, that they also may be in Us, so that the world may believe that you sent me" (NASB). I've observed that in times of desperateness we will sometimes move with love toward each other, where in ordinary times we isolate.

I believe Dr. Lawton's book has many gems of truth we need to consider at this time. Yes, God has made each of us with diversity, but He does not intend for us to be in such disharmony and division. May God challenge us as we try to put the principles of this book into practice.

—Dr. Leland Paris, President,
Youth With A Mission, Tyler (Garden Valley, TX)

Most Christians are familiar with Jesus' prayer in John 17 that all believers would be united as He and the Father were One. Looking around at the Church today, few would suggest Jesus' fervent desire had been fulfilled. Instead, we see the body of Christ broken into thousands of pieces—shattered is not too

strong a word—and hampered from carrying out its mission by disunity.

Merely wishing things were otherwise will not change them. Ecumenism as a concept is tainted with the sense that it involves watering down the gospel. All too often, ecumenism seems to suggest replacing the atoning blood of Jesus with a touchy-feely social doctrine, long on political correctness but short on truth! But the staunchest of believers also fall into error. Some American Christians subconsciously adopt the position that our faith never existed before the last one hundred years . . . and only in the US, at that.

Dr. Lawton's work, *Behind the Shattered Church*, powerfully and effectively answers the question, "How did this fragmentation happen?" Even more importantly, where are there fundamental points of agreement if we are to ever succeed in answering the Lord's assertion that it is by unity that His church will be known?

Reading it will challenge you to look more deeply into the historical roots of your faith. Sharing it with others will open opportunities for dialogue and honest discussion. Studying and praying through *Behind the Shattered Church* will point all of us toward means to heal the wounds in the body of Christ.

—Brock Thoene,
historian and co-author of *The AD Chronicles* and
The Jerusalem Chronicles

BEHIND THE SHATTERED CHURCH

*The Hidden Forces
Separating Us into
Thousands of
Denominations*

By

Willis H Lawton BA, LTh, MD, LMCC

Published by Deep River Books
Sisters, Oregon
www.deepriverbooks.com

This book is published in association with The Benchmark Group Literary Agency, Nashville, TN. benchmarkgroup1@aol.com

Contact the author: willislawton@gmail.com.

ISBN: 9781940269696
Library of Congress: 2015950577

Printed in the USA
Cover design by Jason Enterline

ACKNOWLEDGMENTS

I wish to extend thanks to Jan Rogers, who led the former Woodcrest writing school of Lindale, TX, for training, encouragement, and assistance with the beginning stages of this book.

A special thanks goes to Scott Tompkins, who was on staff at YWAM Woodcrest, for his valuable critique and editing, with unlimited patience, during the multiple rewrites of this treatise. His keen interest in history and theology have been an important asset for communicating the message meaningfully. His encouragement and enthusiasm have made this project an enjoyable experience to the very end.

A very special thanks to my wife, Gail, for putting up with interminable hours of research, reading, and all the writing and rewriting this book has taken. Her support and encouragement have been invaluable.

CONTENTS

CHAPTER 1

FLAGRANT DISOBEDIENCE

The heart of Jesus must be breaking. Day by day, the body he gave his lifeblood to build up is fragmenting like so much broken glass. The thousands of shards may still reflect his light, but not nearly with the intensity that he intended.[1]

In a small western Canadian city there was a thriving interdenominational Christian businessmen's fellowship. The membership was drawn from almost every church in that city, and interchurch relationships were exceptional. Our local president, Bob F,[2] frequently traveled as a speaker to other communities to share his dramatic testimony. At one such meeting, while being introduced, it was mentioned that Bob was Roman Catholic. Immediately over half of the audience got up and walked out.

Because of their religious prejudice, these men missed hearing Bob's powerful testimony of his dynamic conversion and dramatic change of lifestyle. What would you have done? Perhaps, if you are an evangelical, you might question whether it's possible for Bob to be a "born again" Christian while remaining a loyal Catholic. Remember, for those who walked out, their opinions were undoubtedly formed on the basis of what their religious leaders taught concerning what they thought Catholics believed. Might this sort of teaching constitute the sin of gossip?

We've all grown up surrounded by hundreds of different brands of Christian churches, a situation that seems normal since it's all we've ever experienced. These denominational divisions are even interpreted by some as a healthy sign, in that believers have so many "flavors" of church from which to choose. Others see this competition as a sign of strength and innovation. But although competition and innovation fuel the economic world, the Church is not intended to be a business, nor is there any place for a new and improved gospel. And Bob's experience illustrates that there is not just diversity among the many denominations, but also serious division and rejection.

What are the hidden forces that lie behind the shattering of the Church into hundreds or even thousands of independent denominations? Despite growing up in the midst of the denominational multitude, most of us know very little about churches outside our own. We are aware that some have doctrines and worship practices quite different from ours. We likely have been taught that some of those should be avoided, even that they are heretical or demonic in nature. These prejudices go back centuries to times when religious differences often exploded into bloodshed.

Of course, human nature leads us to believe that our own denomination has made all the correct choices concerning doctrine. We are predisposed to think that any possibility of *our* being in error is purely hypothetical. Yet we read in the Bible that Jesus himself prayed for his followers to "be one." Why, we must ask, isn't this high on our priority list?

Miracle in Shellbrook?

In the 1970s, my family lived in the rural community of Shellbrook, Saskatchewan, where I was in medical practice. We had five churches in town, and personal relationships in the ministerial association were amazing. We often socialized with each other throughout the year. Clergy wives met as well for Bible study and prayer.

Within these groups it was decided to have a community-wide mission week. My wife and I were involved in counselor training and the prayer team. Our mission speaker was a Spirit-filled, young Catholic priest. The mission week began in the Pentecostal church for prayer and preparation. Each evening we moved to the next larger church to accommodate growth. Can you imagine a Catholic priest speaking in a Lutheran church about the need to be "born again"? In the Anglican church he taught on the Holy Spirit, and in the Catholic church he taught on healing. The week ended in the large United church with an evening of praise and thanksgiving. The town has never been the same after that. Dozens of Bible studies and prayer groups resulted, and some are still active.

Although I've always been enthusiastic toward the Ecumenical Movement, this experience was a potent energizer. This Catholic priest had mentioned informally to a few of us that he found the Jerusalem Bible to be most valuable in putting Scripture into modern twentieth-century English. It was a fairly new translation at the time. This remark was to eventually have major repercussions.

Several years later, while attending a retreat called Cursillo, a book table with a large Jerusalem Bible caught my attention. I purchased it and still treasure it as my study Bible. This modern translation by the best Hebrew and Greek scholars of the day differs in style from most other Bibles in that it presents the text in one column across the whole page like any other book. Monologues are presented in a narrow central column. While I read the gospel of John, something stood out with astounding clarity. It was the prayer of Jesus just before his arrest. In it we see the urgency of our Lord's own words expressing his vision for his followers:

> ". . . keep those you have given me true to your name,
> So that they may be *one* like us.
> . . . may they all be *one*.
> Father, may they be *one* in us as
> You are in me and I am in you,
> So that the world may believe it was you who sent me.
> . . . that they may be *one* as we are one.
> With me in you and you in me,
> May they be so completely *one*
> That the world will realize that it was you who sent me."
>
> (John 17:11, 21–23, emphasis added)

Notice, the word "one," occurring five times in these few verses, was used in reference to the apostles and those who followed them. The degree of closeness conveyed by the word used here is compared to the unity of the Persons of the Trinity. Though not identical, Father, Son, and Holy Spirit are in complete unity. In his request, Jesus was describing his vision for unity in his Church here on earth. This concentrated emphasis of "one" strengthened my passion to pursue focusing on this will of our Lord for true unity.

The apostles also experienced an urgent intensity in the need for unity. In addressing dissent in Corinth, Paul wrote, "for the sake of our Lord Jesus Christ, make up the differences between you, and instead of disagreeing among yourselves, be united again in your belief and practice" (1 Corinthians 1:10).

He also wrote to the Philippians, "be united in your convictions and united in your love for the faith of the gospel" (Philippians 2:2). Paul knew that competition and division would tear the community apart.

Bodily Unity

How close was this unity intended to be? Paul said, "Now you together are Christ's body; but each of you is a different part of it" (1 Corinthians 12:27). The Church has been known as the "body of Christ" since its very beginning.

> Just as a human body, though it is made up of many parts, is a single unit because all these parts, though many, make one body, so it is with Christ. In the one spirit we were all baptized . . . and one spirit given to us all to drink. Nor is the body to be identified with any one of its many parts. (1 Corinthians 12:12–14)

Here Paul puts the unity Jesus prayed for in perspective. The human body is not a collection of independent pieces like a bag of body parts. All the parts must be organized and connected in order to work together. Foot, hand, and eye have to be coordinated by input from the brain via the nerves to the appropriate muscles in order to walk while carrying something. Sensory input from these parts must return as feedback to the brain to fine-tune the movements.

Our bodies are fearfully and wonderfully made. They are much more complex than Paul, or Darwin for that matter, could ever have imagined. Paul had no idea that the body was composed of cells or how complex these cells were. He had no idea of the DNA helix in the genes, nor the endoplasmic reticulum nor the mitochondria. All these parts in a single cell are involved in producing complex chemical reactions and products. Likewise, we as Christians today have little idea of the complexity of God's design for the Church, including his intention for the parts of it we may disagree with. But God knows it, just as he knows the human body, for he created it for a purpose.

As in the human body, so it is in the church. As baptized persons (in the Early Church baptism was essential for membership) we are integral parts of one living organism. God has a place for each of us and a special role for each one. In order for the Church to function as God planned, we have to be connected to one another and to the head, who is Jesus. When the whole body is listening to the head and cooperating with all its parts, it will function as he intends.

A Military Option

Bob F's experience may give us some insight into why Jesus and Paul cared so much about unity. An ancient strategy is to induce your opponents to fight among themselves, allowing you to divide and conquer. The powers of hell are expert at doing this and frequently attempt to dismember the body of Christ by getting one part to disown the other parts. Sadly, this kind of prejudice can even infect interdenominational groups claiming to be committed to Christian unity. The ploy is to declare the undesired denomination as not being truly Christian. When one church splits off from its parent body to form a new, independent denomination, it is in a true sense dismembering the body of Christ.

This separateness is even evident in small mission communities. I've seen it in Madagascar, in Sudan, and in Peru. In the small villages there often are several denominational ministries all working in competition and isolation from each other.

This competition separates instead of uniting the Christians in these places. Cooperation among them is extremely rare. This separation can't be from God in spite of the excuses offered to justify it. Jesus prayed for us to be one, and the apostles taught oneness as well. When we lose interest in this unity of the whole body, our oneness becomes a backburner issue, but then guess who is cheering?

Considerable research has been done about the growing number of Christian denominations by David Barrett, an Anglican clergyman with missionary experience in Africa. Decades ago, he and his associates examined denominational archives in virtually every country on earth, also studying archives of other religions for comparison purposes. The result was the *World Christian Encyclopedia,* published in 1981 and again in 2001.[3]

The number of denominations they recorded for 1995 was 33,090. That total jumped to 33,909 by the year 2000, and projects that if the same trend continues, there will be 62,262 Christian denominations by the year 2025.[4]

However, this is somewhat complicated by his unique enumeration method. The national total of denominations in each country was multiplied by the number of countries in which each one was found to reach its world total.

For the year 2000, Barrett listed the world population of Christians at approximately two billion. Of these, the Roman Catholic population is over one billion, which is over half of the world's Christians. He also listed the Orthodox Church as having a world population of about 250 million, or approximately one-eighth of the world's Christians. Together, Catholic and Orthodox account for five-eighths of the world's Christians. Barrett's enumeration counted Catholic and Orthodox together as constituting 1023 "denominations" out of the

33,000+ world total.[5] The other three-eighths of the world's Christians account for thirty times as many denominations as both Catholic and Orthodox combined. It looks as if something developed at the time of the Reformation that became the cause of this explosion of denominations.

Strangely enough, Barrett does not believe these huge numbers are indicative of divisiveness. In the preface of the first edition of his encyclopedia in 1981, he writes, "Diversity—divergences in faith and practice from one denomination to another—is not divisiveness; it is what we would expect when Christianity is being spread among some 8,900 peoples speaking 7,010 languages in the world."[6]

Barrett obviously expects the faith to evolve over time and by geography. Yet when the Church is split into hundreds and thousands of independent and competing denominations, God must weep. How can the Church as a whole listen to Jesus, who is the head, when each part is going its own way—and frequently in different directions? At the beginning of the twenty-first century, there were over six billion people on the planet. Of these, one in three was a Christian. What would have happened if all those Christians had the sort of unity Jesus advocated? Would that have changed our effectiveness in reaching out with the gospel to the remaining four billion people on this planet?

Many missionary societies have reported that the Christian faith is spreading very rapidly worldwide, and indeed its population increased from half a billion to two billion during the last century. But review of the increase in the general world population for the same period makes a chill set in: the picture is not as rosy as it might seem.

Referring to a chart in the early part of the *World Christian Encyclopedia,* we find that in 1900 there were 558,131,572 professing Christians, just over half a billion, comprising 34.5 percent of the world population.[7] A century later there were nearly two billion. In the year 2000 that number was 1,999,563,838, comprising . . . only 33.0 percent. A higher number, yes, but a lower percentage. True, the Church was growing by leaps and bounds, but so was the human population. At the beginning of the twenty-first century, there were six billion humans on earth. Less than a dozen years later, this number had grown to seven billion. It is our percentage of this huge number that has the potential to discourage us.

The second most populous religion in the world, Islam, is growing even faster. In 1900 there were 199,940,942 Muslims, who made up 12.4 percent of the world population. This compares to 34.5 percent of Christians at the same time. By the year 2000, there were 1,888,242,789 Muslims making up 19.6 percent of the world population.[8] This compares to 33.0 percent for Christians for the same year. Muslims were up 7.5 percent while Christians were down by 1.5 percent.

Barrett's statistics for the twentieth century could be taken as evidence that Christianity has reached its peak. But in reality, we must ask how much of this sluggishness of Church growth has resulted from interchurch competition.

In Peru, I've seen where Protestant missionaries have worked successfully to convert Catholics, who also believe the Bible to be God's Word. The exposure to enthusiasm over new interpretations of Scripture guided them to switch churches. This is not producing new Christians but moving them from one church to another. Migration of the saints does not reach the unreached! This happens in Protestant churches as well, where Baptists become Pentecostals and Methodists become Lutherans et al. There is a basic problem that is summarized by the saying that "Christianity in America is three thousand miles wide and a half inch deep." Too often we are satisfied with superficial education in the faith. The Early Church frequently required two years of instruction before a new seeker could even be allowed to be baptized. How much instruction do we require to consider a person competent in their understanding of the faith?

Despite these statistics, there are increasing reports from "closed countries" of large numbers of people—especially Muslims—moved by dreams and visions to receive Christ. These conversions could not possibly be counted in the stats, and we should be encouraged that this growth "under the radar" is occurring in spite of our competitive and divisive tendencies.

Yet, if God is supernaturally bypassing the burden of our fractured unity, it does not cancel out our Lord's prayer for unity among Christians. Yet many of us persist in a flagrant disobedience to his will by our insistence on maintaining our divisions. It is urgent that we comprehend the value and significance of the oneness Jesus prayed for. Are we able to awake from this disobedience and open our hearts to the other parts of the body of Christ, even if they are parts we have been taught to reject?

Most Christians claim to believe the Bible and take seriously what it says. The Ten Commandments are always considered sacrosanct, and we usually take seriously the need in John 3:3 and 7 to be "born again." But when Jesus says in John 17 that he wants us to be "one," somehow we don't take him seriously. We urgently need to see why this is so, and to understand the consequences of our choices and what we should do about it.

CHAPTER 2

RADICAL UNITY

Jesus prayed that his followers would have a radical type of unity far deeper than an organizational one. First he prayed "that they may be one like us" (John 17:11). What does it mean to be one like the Father and the Son? It cannot mean being identical or filling the same role, for the Father is not the Son and the Son is not the Father. The Father did not suffer on the cross. Yet, when Philip said, "Lord, let us see the Father and then we shall be satisfied," Jesus replied, "To have seen me is to have seen the Father" (John 14:8–9). In John 14:11 he declares, "I am in the Father and the Father is in me." This is a picture of constant intimacy and interaction. It is that type of unity Jesus envisioned for his followers.

Jesus also prayed, "May they *all* be one" (John 17:21, emphasis added). Here he indicated that he wanted this oneness to include not only the apostles, but all his followers. The same verse goes on to qualify the oneness, describing it as "one in us." It is an interpersonal relationship that defies independence or division. It is a supernatural unity of heart with a purpose that verifies the gospel message, "that the world may believe it was you who sent me." A unity of such supernatural origin would provide a united witness instead of offering the world a cafeteria of "faith opinions."

Usually once a year at least, most churches have prayer for Christian unity. However, there is little or no action taken to pursue it. In this chapter, we want to show how much disunity is present and how it came about. The lack of interest for serious effort reflects an act of disobedience to Jesus. We have to understand just what he meant by this "oneness." First we have to know the meaning of the Church as community as expressed in Scripture.

In the Beginning: Community

Frequently we hear people talk of salvation as "just me and Jesus," but it's clear from Scripture that the Church is not just a collection of isolated individuals but is essentially a community. Creating community was God's idea, which we see in the creation story in Genesis: "God said, 'Let us make man in our image.' In the image of God he created him, male and female he created them" (Genesis 1:26–27). The first humans were physical beings in a physical world, which was the small beginning of community. They were also given a spiritual capacity so they could be interactive with God. This was the beginning of family and of all human community.

Later in Genesis, God called Abraham to leave his father's family and go to a place he would show him. He also promised, "I will make you a great nation" (Genesis 12:12). It was a promise to multiply this one man's family into a "whole people," and it was into this physical nation that God's promised Messiah would come.

When Peter wrote to the Church at large, spread around the Roman Empire, he likened them to a nation: "But you are a chosen race, a royal priesthood, a consecrated nation, a people set apart to sing the praises of God . . . Once you were not a people at all and now you are the People of God" (1 Peter 2:9–10). This picture envisions the Church as a potentially huge community of identifiable people united by their faith in the Lord, like a patriotic nation with the potential to become a whole empire. Muslims refer to themselves as the "Nation of Islam," we are grossly disobedient to be satisfied with our being the independent "city states of God."

The Early Church Fantasy

Surrounded by today's multiplicity of denominations, we rationalize our need to maintain these separations. Invariably in doing so, we pass judgment on one another.

In attempting to avoid "the tradition of man," we might long for the purity of the Early Church. This assumes that evolution of doctrine and practice has been a continuing process since the beginning. It is easy to be convinced that the things we disagree with have evolved away from the original design—and it likewise assumes that the Early Church was in some sense pristine. Evangelical Bible teacher Charles Swindoll has put into words the prevailing view:

> There was no tradition, there were no church constitution and bylaws, no programs, no senior pastor, no "board of elders," no marketing plan, no splinter groups, no corruption—no erosion.[1]

Most who follow this concept think of the Early Church as being pure, simple, and godly, an ideal which we should strive for. However, when we carefully read the Scriptures, we see that Paul shows us what the Church of his day was really like, warts and all. When writing to the Church at Corinth, he referred to them as "the holy people of Jesus" (1 Corinthians 1:2) and then proceeded to deal with problems of disunity and competing factions. In chapters 5 and 6, he dealt with problems of sexual immorality in that same local congregation. In chapters 11 and 12, he dealt with wrongful worship behavior, gluttony, and drunkenness at church, as well as spiritual pride!

It sounds more like a spiritual hospital than our picture of a pristine congregation. This is reality, and it should offer us hope. If such "messed up" people could grow into strong, mature Christians, we should become less judgmental of past ages and of one another's denominations and have hope for restoration even for today's splintered Church.

Why Doctrine Matters

Paul challenged the church at Ephesus to "lead a life worthy of your vocation" (Ephesians 4:1). To this he added, "Do all you can to preserve the unity of the Spirit by the peace that binds you together" (Ephesians 4:2). This is the sort of unity for which Jesus prayed. Paul continued to refer to the whole Church community as consisting of "one body and one Spirit," with the whole Church constituting the "one body of Christ," and being indwelt by the Holy Spirit. He reminds us that there is "one Lord, one faith, and one baptism, and one God who is Father over all, through all and within all" (Ephesians 4:5–6).

Paul's words imply a unity with a set of basic doctrines to be received that is not open to speculation or multiple opinions. Though it is unpopular to talk about doctrine today, doctrine is important because it is the content of the truth which is to be believed.

In Ephesians, Paul then listed five ministry gifts—apostles, prophets, evangelists, pastors, and teachers—"so that the saints together make a unity in the work of service, building up the body of Christ" (Ephesians 4:12). These served to protect from "every wind of doctrine" which had the potential to divide the Church. He also wrote the Church in Corinth, commending them for preserving the teachings of the faith by "maintaining the traditions just as I passed them on to you" (1 Corinthians 11:2). Generally Protestants don't like "tradition," but in reality the Greek word means "that which was passed down." Tradition actually includes the gospel message with its plan of salvation, as well as other details the apostles taught and expected to be passed down. In a sense, Paul meant by "maintaining the traditions" that "we don't mess with the doctrine." He knew this was essential for unity in the Church.

We have seen that Scripture indicates that doctrine and the tradition handed down are important, especially to protect from being led astray. Yet interpretation of that doctrine and those traditions has given rise to contention. Early centuries saw the calling of councils for the whole Church to clarify such doctrines and seal their meaning. In the sixteenth century, individuals felt compelled by conscience to challenge these doctrines and practices. Subsequently, they gained followers and exited the old Church, and as a result, the denominations we know today began.

Doing the Splits

In their book *Unveiling Islam,* the Caner Brothers point out that because of our divisions, Muslims perceive Christians as divided and weak, not only regarding ritual issues but theological issues as well.[2] They see this division as a sign of weakness and corruption. Other non-Christians likely share some of this perception, which has the potential to impede reception of the gospel.

Many Christian leaders who recognize the disunity problem are concerned about at least some of the aspects of division. The evangelical author Francis Frangipane states that "disunity is the work of hell."[3] He cites "confusion . . . concerning church governments"[4] as a cause, with people in the pews unwilling to let the person in charge "be in charge." We will show in a later chapter just what a large role the problem of authority has played in all church division. As dissenters seek to find fault with their leaders, Frangipane contends, "The power reinforcing the inability to reconcile is satanic."[5]

The issues Frangipane sees in the independent, local church, made up of mostly Protestant evangelicals, are more widely applicable to the Church at large, both as having caused divisions in the past and as maintaining them in the present.

A Hopeful Note

Dr. Glenn Wagner, as vice president of Promise Keepers, offered hope for working across denominational lines in his book *The Awesome Power of Shared Beliefs*. He envisioned stimulating unity by focusing on five core beliefs shared by all Christians: 1) the infallibility of Scripture, 2) the deity of Christ, 3) the virgin birth of Christ, 4) Christ's substitutionary death, and 5) Christ's physical resurrection and eventual return.[6] He notes that these "essentials" originate from the time before Church divisions and that the last four are based on the creeds—the Apostles Creed and the Nicene Creed—, which are the Church's most ancient statements of faith.[7] To head these he has added a fifth, the inerrancy of the Bible.[8] Most Christians would be in general agreement with these areas of doctrine, either formally or informally.

If the majority of denominations can agree with these five essentials, then why do we need to remain independent from each other? If all the founders of denominations believed these essential doctrines, one wonders why they were unable to remain with the parent from which they separated. There had to be other factors beyond these minima of the faith which were the cause of the division. Does the Christian faith not contain more doctrines than those expressed in the creeds?

Vagueness of Allusions

Allusions give us partial information. Scripture gives many brief references to aspects of the faith without expressing the full details. Just as the word "Trinity" is neither mentioned nor spelled out in the New Testament, other concepts and practices are also alluded to, such as the "laying on of hands" (1 Timothy 4:14), anointing the sick (James 5:14), and the offices of bishop, deacon, and elder (1 Timothy 3:1–7, 8–12; Titus 1:5–9). All these are mentioned without any details or job descriptions.

Likewise, baptism is frequently mentioned, but without any directions for the procedure. The Lord's Supper is noted in the Gospels but without detail or much doctrine. Paul gave us a few more hints about it in his first letter to Corinth (1 Corinthians 10:15–16, 11:28–30). All these areas are somewhat familiar to most Christians, but because Scripture does not provide detail, the interpretation of doctrines and practices depends on the standards prescribed by the originators of each denomination.

In New Testament times, the apostles themselves taught and demonstrated those details that were not written down in the Bible. For instance, Paul spent from one to three years teaching in the communities he evangelized. He must have taught many details in these time periods as he established the Church in those cities and trained and ordained pastors. Only some of what he did and taught can be gleaned from his letters. Most was oral teaching. The principles underlying the "five essentials" proposed by Glenn Wagner certainly would have been included in Paul's teaching, but they must have comprised only a few of the topics he would have covered.

Without having the details of all the apostles taught, our interpretation of scriptural allusions will defy general agreement. The hopefulness expressed by Glenn Wagner, that the power of what we hold in common will be enough to bring agreement across denominational lines, still falls short of the goal of radical unity because it's the areas we do *not* share that are the problem. Our goal must be to discover and agree on the quality of unity Jesus desires us to seek.

The Character of Unity

We have already seen that the basic concept of human unity began with the family. One man and one woman cooperating in a close, interpersonal relationship are better able to face the challenges of providing food, shelter, and protection. The procreation of children expands that relationship. Love of one another is the integral ingredient of the unity that binds a family together to face the outside world. They are an "us," and everyone else is a "them." Relationship is the essential key.

Families extended become clans and tribes, extending the us/them relationship to develop into nations. Such national unity becomes most visible when people face a common threat. For example, after the attacks on Pearl Harbor and the 9/11 targets, Americans pulled together in unprecedented ways. We gladly sacrificed to support the war effort. Unity and patriotism were at an all-time high. However, the bond of unity in wartime and tragedy are event-centered. As the events fade into history, the once-strong bond of unity dissipates. The character of unity God wants for us is deeper and longer lasting. While it is true that the Incarnation, Crucifixion, and Resurrection of Jesus are historical events, relationship with him is new to each generation. Being "in Christ" and "walking the walk" are present-day realties. Undoubtedly, this is the reason the Church from Pentecost onward celebrated the Lord's Supper weekly, with the intention of continually nourishing that living relationship.

Worship, since the beginning of the Church, has been an essential expression of its unity. Charles Swindoll in *The Church Awakening* focuses on worship. He brings up, in chapter after chapter, the "four principles" of Acts 2:42: the apostles' teaching, fellowship, breaking of bread, and the prayers. This emphasis came from the unity that prevailed at the very beginning of the Church, and it is an example we would do well to emulate today. The "apostolic doctrine and fellowship" of Acts 2:42 potentially opens a way for us to understand the nature of the Early Church and its comparative relevance for us today. However, the breaking of bread, or Lord's Supper, which should be a strong source of unity, has in the last few centuries come to have a changed meaning among most denominations, and it is now a source of bitter disagreement and division. We will look at the reasons for this in a later chapter.

The Body Dismembered?

Young evangelicals and other Protestants have grown up with the understanding that the original unified Catholic Church was corrupt and needed replacement at the Reformation that began with Martin Luther. Since then, the reformed groups have splintered into hundreds of denominations which are accepted as normal in our world today. But what does the Bible say about the Church, and what actually happened in history?

The New Testament pictures the Church as the body of Christ, with all its parts interconnected and functioning in unity. Jesus said that a house divided against itself can't stand (Matthew 12:25). This applies no less to the Church. If we dismember that body, we should expect it be become dysfunctional and lose effectiveness. This is, in essence, what happens when a denomination splits off from its parent.

Those Reformers who led the separation from the old Church to form new denominations did not intend to dismember the body of Christ. They perceived problems in Church leadership and morality that needed serious attention. However, they also misused this situation to justify their rejection of Catholic doctrine and practice which, in fact, had nothing to do with the cause of immorality. They were convinced that the solutions they proposed, and set in motion by separating from the old Church, were of God's leading. Yet, as we shall see, their different leaders chose different paths and doctrines that were sometimes quite incompatible with each other.

The Renaissance and Reformation are often viewed as a period of positive change in the Church, science, arts, government, and education. We easily ignore the negative impact of Renaissance humanism, not only on the Catholic Church, but also on the education of Protestant Reformers. In view of the divisions that followed the Reformation, we may suspect that the Reformers were significantly more influenced by the "New Learning" than we'd like to admit, rather than being totally led by the Holy Spirit.

Our task is now to explore the period between the end of the book of Acts and the advent of Martin Luther to see just what may or may not be found to justify this separation. This is an area of history of which most of us have only a foggy notion. Let us penetrate that fog.

CHAPTER 3

THE FOGGY GAP: EMPIRE PERIOD

Almost all Christians would draw a blank if we asked them, "What happened in the life of the Church between the end of the book of Acts and the appearance of Martin Luther?" This foggy gap in our common knowledge accounts for fifteen hundred of the two-thousand-year existence of the Church. For most of us, very few snippets of information about this era are at all familiar. Yet, crucial events occurred during these centuries that shaped what we believe and practice today. The expressing of basic Christian doctrine in the creeds, the compilation of the New Testament, and the clarification of the structure of ministry, the chain of authority, and worship all happened during the first 350+ years, constituting what I'll call "the Empire Period" of this foggy gap.

A surprising amount of literature was written around the time the Church began as well as over the next few centuries. Copies of these documents, by authors such as Ignatius of Antioch, Justin Martyr, Irenaeus, and the historian Eusebius, have left us considerable documentation of their times. These writings describe the teachings, practices, and authority structure in that Early Church, as well as details of the various attacks on the faith by false teachers. Even a cursory examination of this material will reveal a surprising complexity of doctrine, worship, and authority structures at a very early date. These help us to discern what the Church derived directly from the apostles, as distinct from ideas and theologies from spurious sources of later times.

As the Church spread through the Roman world, it was held together by the ministry and authority structure established by the original apostles. Scripture gives significant detail about the kinds of ministries and authority structure already in use in New Testament days, but we easily risk overlooking them for lack of their being familiar in much of today's church environment. The apostles, who spent three years with Jesus and received instructions from him before he ascended, were the authorities he put in place to have charge over the Church. Within the New Testament, we soon see other kinds of discrete ministries established to supplement their work.

Deacons. With the rapid growth of the Church in Acts, we find a new order of ministry established to look after administrative details and allow the apostles to focus on "prayer and service of the word" (Acts 6:4). Seven men were chosen and ordained by prayer and the laying on of hands (Acts 6:6). They were given the title of deacons, and they looked after details such as the administration of food distribution. Later, Paul, writing to Timothy, recorded the requirements for candidates for this office (or order) of ministry (1 Timothy 3:8–13).

Elders. In Paul's letter to Titus, he told him to appoint elders (*presbuteroi* in Greek and Anglicized to "priests" in English) in Crete as he had been instructed. Paul reminded him of the requirements for the candidates, including "having a firm grasp of the unchanging message of the tradition" (Titus 1:5–9). The gospel message was obviously not intended to evolve! Peter also wrote about elders, saying to them, "Be the shepherds of the flock of God that is entrusted to you" (1 Peter 5:2). The position of "elder" is seen here, in both references, to be essentially that of a pastor to the local congregation.

Bishops. In his letter to Timothy, Paul also gave him the requirements for a candidate for "overseer" (*episcopos* in Greek), or as the King James Version puts it, "bishop" (1 Timothy 3:1–7). Originally this office may have functioned as a kind of "presiding elder" locally, but within a few decades the responsibility became clearly recognized as that of authenticator or guardian concerning the faith that the apostles believed and taught. Within a short time, bishops came to have oversight of more than one local congregation.

In the early decades of the Church, there was probably some overlap of responsibilities among these offices of ministry, but within the next fifty years or so, the duties of each were clearly defined. The Church generally accepted that bishops were considered the successors to the apostles in their function and authority. Even in chapter one in Acts, we find that "the office of oversight," the office of apostle abandoned by Judas, was filled by a replacement named Matthias (Acts 1:20). The King James Version refers to this office as a "bishoprick."

We have seen that there are then three distinct orders of ministry named in the New Testament, along with their qualifications. The Church has historically referred to these orders as the "three-fold ministry" of bishops, priests (elders), and deacons. These offices of ministry remained unchallenged until the Protestant Reformation.

Some modern Protestant leaders, having long ago rejected this original threefold ministry structure, now refer instead to the "fivefold ministry" as listed in Paul's letter to the Ephesians. Here, he lists Jesus' gifts to the Church, whose role it was to build up the Church. They consisted of: apostles, prophets, evangelists, pastors, and teachers (Ephesians 4:11). The trouble is that within a New Testament framework, this can't be shown to apply to any kind of formal Church structure. "Apostles" and "pastors" could conceivably be identified with the offices of bishop and elder, whose qualifications have been noted, but the giftings of prophet, evangelist, and teacher could be applied either to laity or to pastors in charge. Scripture gives no list of qualifications for candidates for prophet, evangelist, or teacher, despite their great value to the Church; nor does it ever command the Church to appoint such people.

It's also interesting to note that one of these five gifts is ascribed to an original deacon. The book of Acts identifies "Philip the evangelist, one of the seven [deacons]." So not only was he a deacon, he had the added gift of evangelist. He had four daughters who were lay members of the congregation but had the gift of prophecy (Acts 21:8–9). Unlike bishops and elders, prophets, evangelists, and teachers are not listed as members of the authority structure of ministry.

New Testament Missions

In Acts, after Stephen was martyred, a bitter persecution ensued. All but the apostles fled Jerusalem (Acts 8:1). These escapees travelled and evangelized in synagogues as far away as Phoenicia, Cyprus, and Antioch, even reaching out to Gentiles. They were the beginning of a first-century "missions movement" that found its fullest expression in Paul and his companions, who established local churches wherever they went and trained and installed leadership. Their journeys were over roads built to serve the military of the Roman Empire, following established trade routes. By road or by sea, one could travel throughout the empire with no threat of war. It was a time called the *Pax Romana*, or "Roman Peace," which benefited the spread of the gospel. Within a century, the Church had been securely established in the territory encircling the Mediterranean.

Entering the Gap: The Church after Acts

It is in Antioch that we get a clearer picture of the structure of Early Church government beyond the New Testament. Tradition has it that Peter went to Antioch, taught, and appointed Evodius as bishop in that city. Evodius was succeeded in that position by Ignatius, the second bishop of Antioch.[1] Ignatius was eventually arrested about 107–108 AD and sent to Rome for execution. He is especially important for us because of the letters he wrote to the Church in the different cities along that journey, only seventy years or so after Pentecost at the beginning of the Church.[2] It is believed that the apostle John, who had now been dead for about a decade, knew Ignatius personally.

The letters Ignatius wrote give us a good window on the organizational structure and teaching at that early date. In these he famously wrote, "Do nothing without the bishop."[3] The bishop in each city was the overseer of the local churches in his area and served as a safeguard against straying from the teaching of the apostles. The warning to "do nothing without the bishop" was to guarantee the authenticity of what was taught in the congregations in his care. This was only about seventy years after the birth of the Church, and the office of the bishop and his episcopal duties were well defined.

Ignatius was also the first on record to use a term which has become controversial only in the last five hundred years. He referred to the Church as "catholic."[4] This term comes from the Greek words *kath holos,* which are literally translated "according to the whole" or "complete," and which may also signify "universal." *Catholic* thus describes the Church as having the faith the apostles had, complete as handed down. The bishop had the responsibility and authority to act as a guardian for this faith, authenticating the teachings for all congregations in his jurisdiction. In a pluralistic world of competing faiths, polytheism, and varying philosophies, such guardianship was as necessary in the first-century Roman empire as it undoubtedly is today.

Countering the Drift of Faith

John was the only apostle to die at an old age of natural causes. Because of this, he was able to teach more than one generation the details of the faith. He settled in Ephesus and lived there most of his life. He traveled to the surrounding areas, including Smyrna, and appointed bishops, reconciled disputes, and performed ordinations.[5] He is probably the one who appointed Polycarp as bishop of Smyrna after teaching him the details of the faith. Polycarp served the Church for eighty-six years until being martyred.

While Polycarp was bishop in Smyrna, Irenaeus, a young lad from a neighboring town, heard him preach on many occasions, recounting what John had taught.[6] This teaching made a profound impression on the young Irenaeus, who as an adult was ordained an elder and later bishop while serving the Church at Lyons, a city in Gaul (modern France).[7] He traveled frequently to Rome and mediated disputes between the Eastern and Western Church. This "Foggy Gap" hero was soon to be instrumental in warning the Church about dangerous heresies.

As the capital of the empire, Rome was a sophisticated cosmopolitan city. It attracted intellectuals with the prominent Hellenistic (Greek) worldview, which presupposed that philosophy was the way to truth. These individuals believed in an underlying dualism where the spiritual was considered good and the material, or physical, world was considered evil. They taught that humans were a mixture of both of these and that salvation was by emancipation of the spirit from the flesh. A high value was therefore placed on asceticism to mortify the body as a sort of subduing of the flesh, which they considered to be evil.[8] Assorted mystery religions with this basic world-view were called Gnostic, because they had a cult secret or *gnosis* which allowed the possessor to "escape the flesh."[9] (By contrast to asceticism, some of these sects allowed the flesh to behave as it pleased, since it was only the spirit that counted.)

About 138 AD, a wealthy young man named Marcion came to Rome[10] and taught in the Church there. He claimed that an inferior deity had created the earth and made humans part-flesh and part-spirit. This deity he identified with the God of the Old Testament, whom he considered bloodthirsty, and should be ignored. The secret good God, Jesus, came to the rescue. He was pure spirit and only appeared to have flesh, since flesh was composed of physical material and was therefore evil.[11] Irenaeus, then bishop of Lyons, was appalled by Marcion and other false teachers in Rome. Their new versions of Christianity prompted him to write a book, *Against Heresies,* in order to expose them. He showed how these teachings differed from the faith that was taught by the bishops, who had a clear lineage back to the apostles themselves. His arguments were probably inspired, at least in part, by his boyhood memory of Polycarp preaching on what John had taught.[12] He argued that the unbroken line of bishops back to an apostle was a guarantee of true teaching. What came to be called the "apostolic succession" was that chain of authentication from bishop to succeeding bishop that verified the faith back to an apostle.

Virtually all false teaching that circulated during the first two centuries of the existence of the Church originated from pagan Greek philosophy. The apostle John warned in a letter, "Keep alive in yourselves what you were taught in the beginning" (1 John 2:24). The gospel did not need a philosophical interpretation to become relevant to the accepted worldviews, and John further warned, "You do not need anyone to teach you" (1 John 2 24–27). This was basically a warning to avoid the philosophy teachers. He also warned that not all that is spiritual is good: "It is not every spirit . . . that you can trust; test them to see if they come from God" (1 John 4:1). "There are many deceivers in the world, refusing to admit that Jesus Christ has come in the flesh" (2 John 7).

To protect against false doctrine, the Church in Rome in the first century began to require those seeking baptism to profess not only that "Jesus is Lord" but also that "he came in the flesh." This required statement was the basis of what was called the "Roman Symbol" (watchword or password[13]) to avoid inviting false doctrine into the Church. This was the early beginning of what eventually became the Apostles Creed, so named for expressing the fundamentals of the faith the apostles had taught.

Continuity of Worship

Continuity of worship was also an important part of the Early Church. In the Jerusalem Church seen in the New Testament, the leaders and people continued going to the Temple for liturgical prayers at given hours, such as Peter and John did in their encounter with the lame man (Acts 3:1). We also see that Paul, at the synagogue in Antioch of Pisidia, was asked "after the lessons from the Law and the Prophets had been read" (Acts 13:15) to speak to the congregation. There was a proper liturgical "order of service" in the temple and also in synagogue worship (liturgy is still used in the synagogue today). A liturgical form is a means of congregational unity for corporate worship. The Catholic and the Orthodox Church today follow a liturgical order with its roots in the Early Church.

In Acts 2:42, the reference to continuing in the "breaking of bread and the prayers" almost certainly indicates the weekly celebration of the Lord's Supper. Paul wrote to the Church in Corinth indicating the solemnity of this meal (1 Corinthians 11:28–30) and also alludes to its doctrine. Very early the name "Eucharist" was applied,[14] which is the Greek word for "thanksgiving."

About fifty years after the death of the apostle John, Justin Martyr, in Rome, wrote a letter detailing how the Eucharist was celebrated each Sunday. He noted that it began with the reading of Scriptures (the Old Testament) and "memoirs of the apostles" (likely the Synoptic Gospels) and preaching on these readings. This was followed by prayer and offering of alms, bread, and wine. A long prayer blessed the bread and wine, and the congregation received communion, which was also taken to shut-ins. Justin Martyr concluded by saying that the blessed bread and wine were no longer considered as common bread and wine, but rather as the body and blood of the Lord.[15] Obviously this ritual was much more complex than many modern church services would have it. Remember this was 155 AD, long before any likely possibility of "evolving away from the New Testament Church" could have occurred.

Legal at Last

Facing adversity and persecution, the Church with its organization of ministry and authority set up by the apostles effectively spread the gospel and became established across the Roman world in spite of being illegal. Up to this time, persecutions were sometimes local and sometimes generalized, but they persisted more than two centuries. The emperor Diocletian in 303 instigated the most severe persecution, which was empire-wide, from Britain to Arabia.[16] Though he abdicated in

305, competition among his four potential successors allowed the persecution to continue until 311.

In 312 Constantine, who was the weakest of the four, backed only by Britain and Gaul, marched into Italy. On the way, he had a vision of a flaming cross in the sky emblazoned with the words *Hoc Vince* (Latin for "by this, conquer"). He understood it as a sign from heaven that God would help him. He then took the Cross as his standard, and soundly defeated the more powerful Maxinius, becoming the sole emperor in the West.[17] In 313, he signed the Edict of Milan, legalizing all religions including Christianity.[18] In 323 Constantine conquered Licinius, his co-emperor in the East, and became sole emperor for the whole Roman empire. From then on, he actively favored Christianity. However, he was not baptized into the Church until near his death. The modern myth that Constantine introduced pagan practice and doctrine into the Church, thus destroying its original "purity," is not consistent with actual history.

A New Heresy

In the early 300s, a priest named Arius, who lived in Alexandria in Egypt, began to teach that Jesus was a created being without prior divine existence.[19] He was a persuasive speaker and gathered a large following, including even a few bishops. Because Christians were now an important part of the population, Emperor Constantine became concerned about this growing division within the Church. He sent a single letter to Alexandria, delivered by Bishop Housius of Cordova, the civil government's religious affairs counselor, from Constantinople. It was addressed to both Arius and to Abba Alexandros, pope in Egypt, requesting that these two come into agreement.[20] ("Pope" was a formal term of endearment for the primary bishop of the area, like "papa.")

At Alexandria, bishop Housius, after much conferring with surrounding bishops, was convinced to agree with Abba Alexandros that this was a severe problem concerning fundamental Christian doctrine. They agreed it would require the collective mind of the apostolic succession, in an ecumenical council of the whole Church, to settle the issue. Contrary to popular opinion, Constantine did not originate the idea of the council, nor did he dictate which side should prevail. It was Bishop Housius who, upon returning to Constantinople, convinced Constantine of the need to call that council to settle the dispute with finality.[21] The date set was June 14, 325 AD, to be held at Nicaea, a port on the Black Sea.

The Council of Nicaea was to have a profound permanent effect on the Church. There were 318 bishops in attendance from various centers around the known world (legend includes one from as far away as Britain).[22] Arius was declared to be in error by the council, and a statement of the true faith was to be drawn up. The committee for its wording consisted of a deacon named Athanasius along with Abba Alexandros of Alexandria and Bishop Leontius of Caesarea of Cappadocia.[23]

The Nicene Creed, as worded at Nicaea in 325 AD

WE BELIEVE IN ONE GOD: THE FATHER ALMIGHTY, MAKER OF HEAVEN AND EARTH: THE VISIBLE AND THE INVISIBLE.

WE BELIEVE IN ONE LORD, JESUS THE CHRIST, THE ONLY BEGOTTEN SON, BORN OF THE FATHER BEFORE ALL AGES; LIGHT OF LIGHT; VERY GOD OF VERY GOD; BEGOTTEN NOT CREATED; CONSUBSTANTIAL WITH THE FATHER; BY WHOM WERE ALL THINGS

MADE; THIS IS HE WHO FOR US HUMANS, AND FOR OUR SALVATION, CAME DOWN FROM HEAVEN, AND WAS MADE MAN BY THE HOLY SPIRIT AND THE VIRGIN MARY; HE WAS INCARNATE; CRUCIFIED UNDER PON-TIUS PILATE, HE SUFFERED, WAS BURIED, AND ROSE FROM THE DEAD ON THE THIRD DAY ACCORDING TO THE SCRIPTURES. HE ASCENDED UP TO HEAVEN AND SITTETH AT THE RIGHT HAND OF HIS FATHER, FROM WHENCE HE SHALL COME IN GLORY TO JUDGE THE LIVING AND THE DEAD; FOR WHOSE KINGDOM THERE IS NO END.

WE BELIEVE IN THE HOLY SPIRIT.[24]

The Council of Constantinople in 381 AD added the final wording about the doctrine of the Holy Spirit, the Church, baptism, and eternal life. The Nicene Creed as now completed is used to the present day in the Catholic, Orthodox, Anglican, and some other churches. It defines the basic standard of core doctrine that is in agreement with the teaching of the apostles. The present-day wording of the creeds will be found in chapter 6.

Prelude to the New Testament

Scripture has always been a key factor in both Judaism and Christianity. Yet, even today there is gross uncertainty among most Christians as to how and when the Church acquired the Bible. In fact, there is *still* some contention as to which books belong in the Old Testament. But there's no need to remain foggy on this all-important point. History is enlightening—and perhaps surprising.

The Bible did not fall from heaven ready-made. The Old Testament had been in use for many centuries and was considered by Jews and early Christians to be "the word of God." The originals had been written in Hebrew and Aramaic, but after the Babylonian captivity, those Jews who settled in places like Egypt lost touch with facility in those languages. They now used the Greek language and lived amid Greek culture. To make the Scriptures more accessible to them, a translation was needed.

Legend has it that Ptolemy of Egypt procured seventy-two scholars from Jerusalem to translate the Jewish Scriptures into Greek in seventy-two days.[25] Two historians from near that time, Philo of Alexandria (20 BC–50 AD)[26] and Josephus (37–100 AD)[27] both support this, though many of today's scholars claim it probably took many translators over several centuries. Whatever precisely its history, the Greek translation is known as the Septuagint or LXX (Roman numerals for seventy) because of the seventy-two legendary scholars. This is the source for the Old Testament used by the Catholic and Orthodox churches. It was from the LXX translation that the apostles quoted in their New Testament references to Old Testament Scripture. The LXX was essentially the standard for the content of the Old Testament for fifteen hundred years for the whole Church until it was shortened to the thirty-nine books accepted by the Protestant Reformation because they did not believe the books now called the Apocrypha, which are included in the LXX, were sufficiently divinely inspired.

The development of the New Testament is a fascinating story. Before there was a New Testament, there were many different collections of Christian writings. The list of acceptable books differed in different places. Generally, most all centers accepted the Synoptic Gospels ("Synoptic" means to "see with the same eye") and read them in church as the "Memoirs of the Apostles" at the Eucharist. The letters of Paul were also read and accepted. Among different lists in the different localities were books such as the Acts of Paul, the Shepherd of Hermas, the Didache, the Revelation of Peter, and the Epistle of Barnabas.[28] Some lists left out Jude and other epistles, as well as Revelation.

For nearly three hundred years after it was written down, there was no full agreement as to the content that should form the New Testament. Christian truth and doctrine were of necessity guarded and affirmed by the succession of bishops. It was forty-two years after the acceptance of the Nicene Creed that the first recorded listing of the twenty-seven books of the New Testament, which all Christians use today, appeared. This list was included in the text of the Thirty-Ninth Festal Epistle of Athanasius of Alexandria in 367 AD.[29]

The nineteenth-century historian Karl Joseph von Hefele wrote *History of the Councils of the Church,* which includes the ecumenical councils like Nicaea as well as lesser, more local such meetings. Among these he examined the Council of Hippo (North Africa) in 393 AD and the Third Council of Carthage (North Africa) in 397 AD.[30] Hefele's work contains documentation of the acceptance of the canon of the New Testament at both of these councils. One report from the Third Council of Carthage declare, "For the confirmation of this canon the church across the sea shall be consulted." The sea was the Mediterranean and the reference is to consultation with Rome.

For the whole Church to achieve agreement on which books were accepted for the canon of Scripture, much prayer was undoubtedly involved, but the councils also needed to employ specific criteria to identify the canonical works, such as being in agreement with apostolic tradition, certainty of apostolic authorship, or acceptance by a Church community that was founded by an apostle. It took from 367 to 397 for many bishops to identify the acceptable books and come to agreement on them, finally closing the canon at the above noted councils.

Today, the New Testament canon is universally accepted by every Christian church and denomination. There is still slight variation in the list of Old Testament books accepted as Scripture in different parts of the Church.

At the time of these councils, the whole Bible was used in the Greek language throughout the Eastern Church. Around 410 AD, St Jerome, using the original texts for the most part, translated the Bible into Latin, which was the language used in the Western Church. This translation was called the "Vulgate" because this Latin was the "vulgar" language, or language of common use.[31]

By the Year 400

By the year 400, the threefold ministry of bishop, priest, and deacon had been the universal practice of the Church for well over three centuries. Along with this was the apostolic tradition, authenticated by the succession of bishops. Liturgical worship had been long established. The Scriptures were in use from the beginning. Previously, the Septuagint essentially had served for the Old Testament, accompanied by the "memoirs of the apostles" and the apostolic letters or epistles. But, the Church now finally had an official, newly accepted, New Testament as well.

At this time, the Christian Church had been legal for nearly a century. Five Patriarchates, headed by leading bishops, were established in the major centers of the Church. These were Jerusalem, Antioch, Rome, Alexandria, and Constantinople.

Though some heretical sects such as Arianism still persisted, there was still only one truly Trinitarian Church, as compatible with the creeds. There were no denominations or divisions, nor would there be for several centuries yet to come. The next struggle was to face the breakup of the empire and wrestle with the anarchy of warlords and the emerging European nationalism that would provide a conflict of interest for Church authority. As the Church entered the next period of the Foggy Gap, it would face some of its greatest challenges yet.

CHAPTER 4

THE FOGGY GAP: MEDIEVAL PERIOD

Following the Empire Period were the Dark Ages (400–1000 AD) and the Middle Ages (1000–1400s), which came to be considered an intellectual void by Renaissance scholars from the viewpoint of Hellenistic culture and learning. Even today we are taught that the Renaissance was a time of true learning that dispelled the darkness and ignorance of ages that preceded it.

However, intellectual activity continued during this period, and contrary to the myths that see the Church as the center of ignorance during this time, it was the Church that drove learning—as evidenced by the founding of monasteries that preserved learning through the establishment of libraries and the copying of Scripture and other books and manuscripts. In the late twelfth and thirteen centuries, in the universities, Scholastic philosophers made their mark by using the Greek philosophy of Aristotle to the expressing of the faith.

Even so, it was in this one thousand year period that significant forces and events arose that directly fueled the Protestant Reformation. The Roman empire was beginning to crumble, resulting in political turmoil that compromised the Church's freedom and quality of life. A struggle for authority ensued between Church and government, later followed by the pressure of rising Hellenistic intellectual influence on Western culture.

The Beginning of the End

On the borders of the empire, barbarians were increasing in strength. Germanic tribes called Visigoths sacked Rome in 410 AD. By default, Innocent I, as bishop of Rome, took charge of relief and rebuilding the city after the attack. As attacks continued throughout many Roman provinces, the bishops, being the most educated and reliable people in these areas, were called upon to assume the duties of imperial officers and judges and even to function as governors, using their influence to protect the populace.[1] In 455, when the Vandals attacked Rome, Pope Leo I negotiated with them not to burn the city or kill its inhabitants and limit their plundering to a fortnight.[2] When Attila, leading the Huns, invaded Gaul in 451 and got into northern Italy, Pope Leo I successfully negotiated with him to spare Rome.

The empire continued to survive for another twenty-five years, but it fell in 476 when a Germanic Roman army general deposed the last Western emperor.[3]

After Rome fell, the Church was the only remaining stable entity in the West, and because of this, it was conscripted into civil governmental duties. This union of Church and State was not entirely a happy one. The warring tribes north of the old imperial borders continued to vie for power for the next few centuries. The successful ones formed powerful kingdoms.[4] Such was the case for the pagan warlord Clovis (481–511). Though he converted to the Catholic faith, he and his heirs kept a tight grip on the Church in his domain. They even required that a man get their permission before he could become a clergyman. They sold Church positions and rigged the election of bishops to their liking.[5] Such interference by the governing ruler diluted the faith and introduced a new worldliness into the Church, which eventually led to the loosening of morals among the clergy.

Decades after the fall of the Western empire, the Eastern emperor Justinian I (527–565) attempted to restore the old Roman empire with Constantinople as its sole capital, but he had little success.[6] He knew theology, and he claimed control of the Church to be part of his mandate, including selecting bishops, calling councils, and amending canon (Church) law.[7] The Western Church was sufficiently distant as to be more independent and noncompliant with the Eastern emperor's agenda. Justinian did succeed in founding and financing monasteries, hospitals, and churches. To help resist paganism at the source of its intellectual strength, he closed the ancient schools of philosophy at Athens in 529 AD.[8]

Rising Lights

While the "Dark" descended on Europe, new light was beginning to rise at the "ends of the earth," namely in Ireland. To serve the few Christians along Ireland's east coast, Pope Celestine I sent Palladius as bishop for them.[9] The man we now call St Patrick was probably among his assistants. Patrick was helpful, knowing the language and customs of the Irish after being a kidnapped slave in Ireland for six years in his youth, followed by a call to return to the island and evangelize its people. Palladius died after a year, and Patrick was made bishop in 432. He evangelized extensively and established monasteries throughout Ireland.[10] By around 600 AD, Ireland had become the cultural leader in Europe.[11] From there, St Columba founded a monastery on the isle of Iona and daughter houses in Gaul and Italy, and he helped evangelize the Lombards, barbarians from the area of East Germany who had invaded Italy.

Another light was Benedict of Nursia (480–543),[12] who as a youth studied in Rome but was disgusted by the vice and frivolity of the city. Between ages of fifteen and twenty he became a hermit. Later, realizing the dangers of solitary life, he developed a "Rule of Life" for living in community that would become widely influential for religious communities.

In 528–529, Benedict moved to Monte Casino and established a monastery. Though never ordained, he was consulted by priests and bishops. His "Rule" became the standard for Western monasteries, with its emphasis was on prayer, work, and study. His monasteries were self-supporting.[13] He began schools for literacy which included boys and girls age seven and up. He housed political exiles, and with the decline of towns, the monasteries became the most densely populated places in Europe.[14]

With the failure of imperial government, we've already seen how the Church was called to help fill the gap through negotiation and protecting the people. In Rome, the extraordinary Pope Gregory I ("Gregory the Great," 590–604) was a bishop who bore such civil responsibility but also successfully maintained his spiritual duties. He provided relief for the poor in Rome as well as maintaining public works and managing Church lands. These he managed so efficiently as to increase revenue and working conditions for peasants. He even raised an army to protect Rome.[15] Not only did Gregory keep Rome safe, but was also a reformer and teacher of the faith. It was he who sent Augustine of Canterbury to Britain to reevangelize England, which had been overrun by pagan barbarians who had severely attacked the faith.[16] He is also noteworthy for participating in liturgical reform and Church music. He promoted "Gregorian Chant," a style of liturgical singing that can still be heard today. He was an active preacher and a believer in miracles, and he maintained discipline among clergy.[17]

A New Dynasty and New Threats

From 500–1000, there was a slow decline in the world population of Christians.[18] Part of the cause was a new, aggressive religion, Islam, which originated in Arabia in the early seventh century. Islam's military conquests and subsequent conversions advanced across what till now had been Christian North Africa and on into southern Europe, as well as to Persia and the borders of India and China. Charles Martel ("the Hammer"), heir to the throne of the Frankish kingdom of the "Holy Roman Empire," successfully rose to meet the threat. In 732, the Islamic Saracens under Abd-ar-Rhan advanced into Gaul and burned Bordeaux. Charles then soundly defeated him at Poitiers, terminating the advance of Islam in Europe.[19]

Charles Martel was a hero in his day, but his rise precipitated a new twist in the European competition for authority. Martel was a strong supporter of missionary activity in Germany. The most famous of these missionaries was St Boniface, who cut down the Oak of Thor, which the pagan Germans worshipped as a god. Subsequently, Boniface was made an archbishop by Pope Gregory III in 732.[20] Later, Boniface precipitated a watershed event by anointing Charles's son "Pepin the Short" as king.[21]

The significance of that event can't be overstated. Up until then, the imperial thrust had always been to have the Church under its control. The acceptance of anointing by a bishop along with crowning was a symbolic concession by the state to submit to the spiritual authority of the Church. (The significance goes back to the Old Testament, where the prophet Samuel, representing the authority of God, anointed Saul and later David as king.) The receiving of such an anointing was a recognition that royal authority was from God and was now being conferred by the Church.

This affirmation of the spiritual authority of the Church over the state continued when Pepin's son Charles, better known to us as Charlemagne, was anointed and crowned Emperor of the Holy Roman Empire on Christmas day 800 AD by the pope.[22]

Like his father and grandfather before him, Charlemagne recognized the need for better education for the clergy so they could more effectively teach the faith to the people, and he encouraged bishops and abbots to set up schools to accomplish this.[23]

Conflict of Interest: Feudal Complications

Throughout the medieval era, the feudal pattern of government prevailed in the West. Because of the absence of strong central government, civil order depended on personal interdependent relationships.[24] The authority of a king, petty or major, depended on the loyalty of his nobles, who held their land ("fiefs") as vassals in chief under the king. These in turn had vassals under them, holding lesser fiefs as lesser lords of the land.

Bishops, as holders of Church lands, were torn between the demands of the Church and the need to please the nobles above them. The land was the fief which they, as vassals, held in stewardship. The nobles wanted everyone in their domain to be loyal and trustworthy to them, which was the reason behind their attempt to control the Church. A noble could ensure such loyalty of Church leadership by rigging the selection of a bishop to be one of his own henchmen, even if he had faulty spiritual qualifications. Such conflicts of interest for bishops plagued the Church for the duration of the feudal system.

The continuing conflict of loyalties compromised both spirituality and morality in the Church despite sporadic efforts to reform the situation. Pope Gregory VII (1073–1085) issued a decree in 1075 forbidding lay investiture, hoping to regain some spiritual control in the Church. He insisted that only bishops should invest a new bishop with his badges of office, thus maintaining the proper perspective on the line of authority in the Church.[25] The Germanic king of the Holy Roman Empire, Henry IV, disobeyed, presenting a new bishop with his Crook and Ring—an act of lay investiture. For his flagrant disobedience, Henry was excommunicated. He eventually repented and stood barefoot in the snow for three days where the pope was in residence. Pope Gregory gave him absolution, restoring him to the Church.[26] This helped reset a further precedent for recognition of the spiritual authority of the Church over that of the secular world and reinforced the need for separation of Church and state. The Church needed the primary obedience of the clergy so they would be first of all churchmen rather than pawns of the state.

The First Church Split

Meanwhile, the Islamic control of the Mediterranean, as well as much of the territory surrounding Constantinople, made it difficult for the Roman see and the Eastern patriarchates to communicate and resolve Church disputes about authority and doctrinal issues. In 1054, the differences escalated to the point that the pope and the patriarch of Constantinople excommunicated each other.[27] The other three Eastern patriarchs stood with Constantinople, comprising what we know today as the Orthodox Church. The Western Church, having almost identical orthodox theology, is known as the Catholic Church.

This schism, or Church split, was almost resolved in May 1274 at the Second Council of Lyons and unity was declared to be restored. But international politics prevented its implementation. Further unsuccessful attempts were made in 1369 and 1493.[28] Pope John Paul II had dreamed of succeeding with unity in time for a joint celebration of the Eucharist by both Orthodox and Catholic Churches to greet the new millennium in 2000 AD, but so far the schism persists.

The Crusades

Islam, meanwhile, was continuing to grow using military means. The Eastern Empire came under increasing stress from continuing Islamic conquests. The Seljuk Turks conquered most of Asia Minor (modern Turkey) before the end of the eleventh century. This whole land had been Christian since the time of St. Paul. These invaders occupied Jerusalem in 1071 and took Antioch in 1085.[29] Overtures were made by the Eastern emperor to Pope Gregory VII for aid, but although he sympathized and planned a Crusade to rescue the Eastern Empire, it never materialized.

In 1094, the Eastern emperor Alexius (1081–1118) sent envoys to Pope Urban II asking for help.[30] The request met with enthusiasm, and by 1096 the first Crusade set out. At first there were waves of poorly organized groups, some of whom even attacked Jews and fellow Christians along the journey.[31] A better organized wave arrived in Constantinople that winter and recaptured Antioch in 1098 and Jerusalem in 1099.

The Crusaders experienced some friction with Alexius, who had only wanted aid to recover the provinces lost to the Muslims. Indeed, they did recapture Nicaea and return it to him in 1097. But some of them had a hidden agenda, which was to conquer Palestine and create their own dominion.[32] The first

Crusader state was Edessa, beyond the Euphrates. Encroaching on the jurisdiction of the Eastern Patriarch, Rome appointed a Patriarch of Jerusalem as well as other bishoprics, extending the Western Church into the East.[33] This increased the stress on the East/West schism rather than helping to heal it.

A second Crusade set out in 1144 to deal with the fall of Edessa, but the Kurdish Saladin prevailed, and by 1187 the Crusaders were defeated.[34] A third Crusade in 1189 included Fredrick Barbarossa of the Holy Roman Empire, King Philip of France, and Richard the Lionhearted of England. Fredrick died en route; Richard and Philip quarreled. The only result was the recapture of the port of Acre.[35] A fourth Crusade set out in 1204, but instead of advancing against the Muslims, it conquered and plundered Constantinople, the seat of the Eastern Empire. Other Crusades continued but fell far short of honorable goals. Jerusalem fell to the Muslims in 1244 and remained in Islamic control till the twentieth century.[36] What at first seemed a laudable enterprise fell far short of the Christian ideal of reaching the nations for the Lord. Because the Church employed the cultural, secular means of military aggrandizement, the Crusades left a black mark on the history of the Church.

Babylon and the Great Schism

About this time, political enmity between Italy and France drew the papacy into its conflict. This had serious implications for fueling the Protestant Reformation. For his safety, the French-born Pope Clement V moved from Rome to Avignon in 1309 for fear of attack by Italian patriots, and he supervised the Church from there. A chain of seven popes made Avignon their home base until 1377.[37] This period was called the "Babylonian Captivity of the Church" by Italians and others because the Bishop of Rome was located in the French city of Avignon instead of in Rome. The likeness to the Jews being in Babylon instead of Judea during the captivity did not escape them. In 1377 Gregory XI returned to Rome, but he died within a year. The cardinals, mostly French, were under pressure to elect an Italian to replace him. They elected one, from Napoli, as Urban VI. The cardinals then left Rome, repudiated Urban, and elected Clement VII to replace him back in Avignon.[38]

The problem at this time was not a split in the Church, but rather a national political dispute between France and Italy. Both wanted the Chair of Peter to be located in the territory of their control. Having rival popes did not create competing churches, but rivals claiming to be the pope of the one Catholic Church. Each of the European countries favored their own choice of which one they thought was the true leader. Some countries supported Urban and others supported Clement.

The plan, proposed by Scholars, was made for the two claimants to resign and be replaced with a new pope. At the Council of Pisa in 1409, Alexander V was elected, but he died within a year, and John XXIII was elected to replace him.[39] All three claimed the chair of Peter, and no one stepped down. Finally in 1417 the Council of Constance succeeded in getting the three to step down and elected Martin V as the one pope.[40]

(There may be some confusion surrounding the name Pope John XXIII. The one referred to above was one of the disputed popes, and therefore the choice of that name and number was still available for our modern Pope John XXIII, who called Vatican II in the 1960s.)

The period between 1378–1417 is officially known as the Great Schism and was purely about the politics of power between Church and state. No changes were made to the doctrines or traditions of the Church. The significance of all this was the proposal of a conciliar movement to create an authority superior to the papacy.[41] Concerned Scholars at the University of Paris and some others hoped to call a general council like Nicaea that would have authority above that of the pope. This movement did result in calling the councils of Pisa and Constance, but they did not achieve the hoped-for conciliar authority. Nevertheless, the push for a conciliar power over the papacy served to encourage the later protesting Reformers to attack the legitimacy of papal authority.

A Crisis of Worldview

The historian Previte-Orton identified a Renaissance[42] as early as the 1100s in the West, where an increasing interest in ancient science as well as literature was beginning to flower. Much of the material feeding this interest came from Muslim translations of Greek into Arabic which was later translated into Latin by Jewish scholars in Spain.[43] Latin translation was needed to make these materials accessible again, since facility with Greek had been absent in the West for many centuries.

The twelfth and thirteenth centuries were blessed with many translators, particularly in the areas of mathematics, medicine, and astronomy. Mathematics as a discipline was also taking on new force, greatly benefitting by the introduction of Arabic numerals that had been invented in India.[44]

One legacy of the Crusades was an acceleration of the influx of classical literature, art, and philosophy into the West. In 1204, a Crusade consisting of Latin membership facilitated direct interaction with Greeks, which aided the translation of Aristotle and other philosophers into Latin.[45] However, this cultural and intellectual flow into the West precipitated a new danger for the Church by promoting subtle changes of worldview. More than military endeavors or even the divided loyalties of feudalism, the coming shift in worldview would bring about crisis for the Church.

In the age of the Early Church Fathers, in the second and third centuries, philosophy was studied but was primarily intended to help express the faith. The presupposition was that the gospel was true, and the concepts of philosophy provided some useful ways to express what the Church taught from its tradition. As the Renaissance approached, a shift had occurred. Renaissance humanist scholars now began with the presupposition that philosophy was the standard of truth, and they employed it to judge the Church. In this way, the Renaissance called into question the traditions of the Church and ultimately its doctrine and authority.

This new cultural milieu was facilitated by the growth of commerce and economic improvement in city life, which allowed leisure for the middle and upper classes to pursue art and literature. As the Middle Ages waned, the city of Rome, like Florence and other major cities in Europe, was increasingly marked by a worldly decadence, perhaps even more so for having been the former capital of the empire. The sophisticated populace of such centers was receptive to the hedonistic side of Greek philosophy, art, and literature that had flowed increasingly in from the East for several centuries now.

With its fascination with this intellectual flood, the Renaissance produced a change of values, introducing a system of thought that questioned everything and sought its fulfillment in human achievement. It minimized the role of God and the need for redemption and eternal life. Instead, this new system of humanism fostered a spirit of independence and pride, tending to ignore morality in its exuberance for life in this world.[46]

Prior to the rise of universities, medieval centers of learning were concentrated in monasteries, providing Christian teaching and literature as well as preserving ancient learning. Not only were they providing theological education, but monks tediously copied and stored many ancient manuscripts as well as Scripture.

But now, municipal centers of "new learning" became the seed of universities. The Universities of Paris and Bologna became major universities over the centuries to come. The earliest university was in Salerno, where Greek, Latin, Arabic, and Jewish cultures converged. It was here in the tenth century that a famous medical school was founded.[47] Bologna, by the thirteenth century, offered a doctorate in civil and canon law as well as in arts and medicine.

Originally, universities grew out of the Christian thrust for education. However, the teaching of Greek philosophy, such as that of Aristotle, at first worried the Church. Prelates were appalled at the thought of heathen speculative philosophy coming into a Christian university.[48] The faculty, however, welcomed it. Thomas Aquinas (about 1276) and Albert of Cologne (about 1280) were both Christian teachers at the University of Paris, where they attempted to use philosophy as support for the faith as did Early Church Fathers and "make Aristotle intelligible to the Latins."[49]

Infecting the Church

During the majority of feudal times, the Church was under the powerful control of princes and nobles and was only sporadically able to carry out some of the reforms it recognized as necessary. By the close of the Middle Ages, it had gained sufficient power and freedom to complete the reforms. Unfortunately, the insidious advance of secular humanism from the pagan classics had begun infecting the Church, many of whose prelates were becoming caught up in the "new learning." The influence of the pagan classics even touched the papacy.

Nicholas V (1447–1455) is considered the first Renaissance pope. He studied at Florence, the epicenter of the Renaissance, and attempted to combine humanism with Christian principles.[50] He benefited the Church by founding the Vatican Library to preserve valuable books and manuscripts. On the other hand, he tried to make Rome the center for new humanist art and recruited humanists to serve his cultural endeavors who were essentially pagans.[51]

He was followed by Callistus III (1455–1458), who filled Church positions with relatives.[52] He was followed by Pius II (1458–1464), who focused on the Turkish military threat.[53]

Paul II (1464–1471) was anti-humanist and a bit of a reformer. He attempted to expel the more pagan of the humanists from Rome and stop the selling of Church positions, which had been a practice off and on during the Middle Ages.[54]

Pope Sixtus IV (1471–1484) was a humanist supporter who enlarged the Vatican Library. He began building the Sistine Chapel, which is named after him. His dream was to make Rome the literary and art capital of Europe.[55] Innocent VII (1484–1492) became pope when morals were abysmal in the general population and even in the Church. He sold Church offices and created new ones to sell.[56]

Next came Rodrigo Borgia as Alexander VI (1492–1503), whom many historians consider the lowest point of the papacy.[57] He is reported to have had a mistress who was married three times, and together they had seven children.

At this point in history, the Church reflected the lowered moral standard of the times. Instead of being salt and light in the world, the deeply compromised Church was going with the flow—it was no worse but no better than the rest of the culture. Yet even in this era there were bishops and others who, taking their faith very seriously, felt an urgency to correct the abuses. They sought to end greed and corruption and return to the true practice of the faith. After all, it was not the teaching of the Church, nor its doctrine, which caused the corruption; rather it was the ignoring of these which permitted the spiritual compromise.

The Renaissance was a time of intense intellectual ferment, bringing many new ideas which opened the door to challenge the very authority of the Church. This served to facilitate the unfolding of the Protestant Reformation.

The Renaissance culture in Italy was a changer of culture throughout the West. The "New Learning" captured the hearts of especially the upper classes, which included bishops, in a way that was much like our present-day American culture becoming more extremely "liberal" and focused on the less moral arts and literature. This new culture also provided an intellectual liberalism that challenged the "old-fashioned" morals and religion. Young students eagerly questioned the validity of the Church and its authority. Intellectual meanderings from there eventually gave individuals permission to question and change the Church. This entire trend may feel familiar in that is our situation today, both in government and often in church. Philosophy was big on the cultural landscape, and Church unity was displaced from prominent interest.

CHAPTER 5

THE PROBLEM OF AUTHORITY

The problem of authority is the problem of "who is in charge?" If we just mention the word *authority* when talking about the Catholic Church, it usually turns to a discussion about the pope. Protestants often consider him as an absolute monarch ruling all Catholics like a despot. This attitude didn't come from nowhere: the author Karl Adams, in describing the writings and attitude of Martin Luther toward the authority of Rome, says, "He converted opposition and even hatred towards the Papacy into an essential element of Protestantism."[1] This "absolute monarch" understanding of papal authority persists among many Protestants even today. Actually the pope is a bishop, and as bishop of Rome, is essentially the "chief pastor." Authority in the Catholic Church is vested in three spheres, "the ministry" (bishops and the apostolic succession), "the tradition of the apostles," and the Bible. These three, of necessity, must be in agreement. This provides stability, such as we read in Scripture: "and a threefold cord is not quickly broken" (Ecclesiastes 4:12).

All the stresses and divisions that have plagued the Church, stem from perceiving authority as simply "the power to coerce." This understanding of authority has also played a prominent role in the denominational splintering that began during the Protestant Reformation, and it continues to do so today. Our negative reaction to authority is a feature of our cultural heritage, derived from the Renaissance and Enlightenment philosophy that encouraged the pride of human intellect and the spirit of independence. Growing up in America, we learn to cherish a spirit of independence and detest anyone making demands or messing with our freedom. Our school systems teach about the American Revolution and the French Revolution, directing our sympathies toward the rebels, who were the heroes who won over the "tyrannical kings." Even modern news media, reporting on political turmoil, tends to encourage sympathy with the rebels.

The normal response to feeling coerced is to rebel. This is what provided the inspiration to question the validity of Church authority and its doctrine. The cultural perception developed that authority by its very nature and existence was "infringing on our rights." But in this way, it might be said that the feeling of coercion is in the eye of the beholder.

An "independent spirit" encourages authority to be placed in the autonomous local church rather than coming from external oversight. All modern independent churches, as well as many denominational churches have their governing authority vested in a local church board whose decisions are made by democratic vote. How "church is to be done," what doctrine is acceptable and what is not, and even whether to hire or fire the pastor depend on a vote by board members, who are normally elected by the congregation. In essence then, authority would appear to be derived from the congregation and delegated through the board—"of the people, by the people, for the people." Are the sheep leading the shepherd? Rather than following a biblical precedent, this is compatible more with the authority system of a republic, reflecting a latent Renaissance influence. However, the Church is part of a kingdom and not of a republic.

Authority operated differently in the New Testament. The apostles were in charge, being the ones with the "message."

They were the authorized experts about the gospel, having been with Jesus for three years and receiving their authority from him. They in turn imparted this authority to their successors. This is the pattern that has continued in the Catholic and the Orthodox Churches to the present.

What Is Authority?

What we understand by "authority" is colored by our culture and emotions. The dictionary definitions of authority fall into two general areas.[2] The first is "the right to coerce obedience," and the second is that of "the knowledge of the expert." The right to coerce obedience can be exercised by using laws and force to compel obedience, or this "right to coerce" can be exercised by invitation as we see it lived and taught by Jesus, namely "servant leadership." This is essentially "coercion by attraction" rather than by using force, in that the obedience is voluntary even while the authority has a right to it.

Jesus told his disciples, "Among the pagans their so called rulers lord it over them . . . this is not to happen to you . . . anyone who wants to be great must be your servant" (Mark 10:42–45). John tells us that when Jesus washed the disciples' feet, he said, "I have given you an example so that you may copy what I have done" (John 13:15). Keep in mind that an authority who serves does not relinquish authority but rather it is the manner in which that authority is exercised. Servant leadership does not force obedience, but invites it through loyalty of the heart so that we desire to obey. The internalization of the values taught and modeled help us control our behavior from the inside, even when "Big Brother" is not watching.

Christians will agree that the authority to command and enforce obedience rightly belongs to God as Author and Creator. Because of his nature and character, we should not be surprised that he would share some aspects of authority, as we see happening when Jesus delegated authority to his disciples. However, it is important to understand how authority is to be legitimately delegated. The creation story says that God created humans in his own image and gave them authority to rule over fish, birds, cattle, and all life forms (Genesis 1:26–28). This was not simply a privilege, but an assigned responsibility.

Scripture later indicates that this authority is not limited to plants and animals but is to be exercised over other humans too, especially in the form of civil government. Paul says that we must obey the government because all civil authorities were "appointed by God" (Romans 13:1–2). He goes on to say that to resist authority is "rebellion against God's decision." Such words should make us uncomfortable when we tout devotion to our spirit of independence.

Further, Scripture indicates that governing authority needs to be authorized. The prophet Samuel was directed by God as to whom to anoint king (1 Samuel 9:61). In the next chapter he anointed Saul, which expressed the seal of divine approval and authorizing the delegation of such civil authority from God to the king. All the tribes of Israel officially accepted Saul as their king. Later, Samuel in like manner anointed David as the next king (1 Samuel 16:13). This was the precedent for anointing and crowning kings and emperors in past ages and is presently still part of the installation of the British monarch, whom the Archbishop of Canterbury anoints in this ritual.

To grasp authority without proper authorization is an act of rebellion. In Leviticus 10, we read the story of Aaron's sons, who suffered severe punishment for seizing authority that had not been given to them: "Nadab and Abihu, sons of

Aaron, each took his censer, put fire in it and incense on the fire, and presented unlawful fire before Yahweh, fire which he had not prescribed for them" (Leviticus 10:1–2). Later, when Saul took the authority to offer sacrifice upon himself—something only Samuel was authorized by God to do—his excuse was, "The Philistines are going to fall on me at Gilgal and I have not implored the favour of Yahweh. So *I felt obliged to act and I offered the holocaust myself*" (1 Samuel 13:12, emphasis added). Samuel's reply was "you have acted like a fool," and he pronounced the coming end of Saul's dynasty because of his disobedience.

A later king also took authority into his own hands. Uzziah, "as he prospered, grew proud" and decided to burn incense on the altar of incense in the Temple. Eighty priests resisted his efforts, saying, "It is not for you to burn incense to Yahweh, but for the priests, the sons of Aaron, consecrated for the purpose" (2 Chronicles 26:18). Uzziah's presumption earned him leprosy. One could ask whether this biblical principle might have significance for the challenges to Church authority and the establishment of new doctrines and forms of ministry in the sixteenth century? How were the Reformers authorized, and by what permission?

Though the very asking of questions like this will make many readers extremely uncomfortable, yet they are worth asking. The particular historical viewpoint we have unquestionably accepted has somehow led to a situation which is very different from the unity for which Jesus prayed. If we desire to be honest about it and are willing to seek a remedy, it is necessary to revisit the events and choices of the past with a fresh, cool mind. From there we may be able to come to understanding and find the course forward.

Early Reform and Reformers

A medieval "self-authorization" occurred in France in 1170 AD when a pious but untrained merchant we know as Peter Waldo felt moved to espouse poverty and share his faith. He convinced some priests to translate portions of the Bible into French. He gathered followers, and his band of "Poor Men of Lyons" was at first approved by Pope Innocent III, on the condition they obtain permission of local clergy to preach. Waldo felt this infringed on his call to preach and rebelled instead. He then denounced the clergy, finally earning condemnation by the Council of Verona in 1184.[3] He rationalized his rebellion by claiming the Bible to be the only authority he would obey. Because of this stand, most Protestants consider him a hero of the faith. His many followers dispersed into many varieties of doctrine and eventually went into exile, and some of them still exist today.

In contrast to Waldo, another pious layman we know as St Francis of Assisi (1181–1226) had a religious experience in 1209 which he considered as a call to espouse poverty and become a travelling preacher. He gathered barefooted followers who preached and helped peasants do their field work. In 1210, he and eleven followers went to Rome and obtained permission from Pope Innocent III to become a religious order on the condition they appoint a "Superior" and obtain permission from the local bishop before preaching.[4] Unlike Peter Waldo, Francis and his "Franciscans" were obedient to the conditions of authority. Consequently they flourished and preached, and the order continues their work to the present.

New Testament Authority

Before he ascended, Jesus told his apostles, "All authority in heaven and on earth has been given to me" (Matthew 28:18).

Then he assigned them to go with his authority to all nations to make disciples. Though he had given authority to them, he instructed them to wait in Jerusalem for the Holy Spirit to energize what he had imparted.

Previously, Jesus had sent the Twelve out in pairs after imparting to them authority over unclean spirits, and they had cast out devils and healed the sick (Mark 6:7–13). Similarly, he had sent out the seventy two, also in pairs, who did a similar ministry by his authority (Luke 10:1–20). None of these just decided to take on authority for themselves—Jesus specifically imparted it to them.

Jesus asked the disciples who people said he was. After several answers were offered, Peter came up with the correct one—that Jesus was the Christ. Jesus told him it was not by human reason but by divine revelation that he knew this. He then said to Peter (speaking in Aramaic), "So now I say to you: you are *kepha,* and on this *kepha* I will build my Church . . . I will give you the keys to the kingdom of heaven: whatsoever you bind on earth shall be considered bound in heaven; whatever you loose on earth shall be considered loosed in heaven" (Matthew 16:16–19). The literal reading of these words indicates he gave Peter a unique place of authority in the Church, as symbolized by giving him the "keys."

Some argue that the "rock" (kepha) was not the man given the keys, but rather that the words Peter said about Jesus were the rock. Therefore, detractors claim, Peter did not (and his descendants do not) have any right to "rule" over the church. This suggests a misunderstanding of the manner of authority involved. Neither Peter nor the apostolic succession he authorized in Rome were to "lord it over" the Church, but they were to follow the foot-washing example. It was the "authority of the expert" for the purpose of authenticating the gospel message and sharing it, rather than just the message alone.

A Catholic view, in a report by Cardinal Ratzinger from a symposium in 1996, reads, "The successor to Peter is the rock which guarantees a rigorous fidelity to the Word of God against arbitrariness and conformism."[5]

When Jesus delegated authority to Peter (Matthew 16:16–19), it was to be exercised by invitation, in servant leadership. Early on, in about 180 AD, Irenaeus, Bishop of Lyons, was fighting heresies by appealing to the true faith as preserved and passed down by the bishops in apostolic succession. He wrote, "It is a matter of necessity that every church should agree with this Church,"[6] referring to the Church in Rome, in apostolic succession from Peter. At that early date, his understanding of authority involved leadership and authentication of the gospel message and Christian doctrines. This was an early recognition of the "primacy of Peter," which has been supported in the Western Church from early times and to a lesser degree in the Eastern Church.

The Authority of Authentication

An expert is one who is competent to convey true facts or carry out a specific skill. The apostles were the obvious experts concerning the Christian faith, able to guarantee the truth of what they taught by their personal experience with Jesus. In order to carry the gospel to all nations, it was necessary for them to teach others to become fully competent so as to be able to be placed in authority, and to likewise guarantee the authentic faith was passed down. This is the basis of the concept of apostolic succession.

We see this delegation of apostolic authority clearly happening in New Testament times. Paul wrote Titus in Crete,

"Appoint elders in every town, in the way that I told you" (Titus 1:5), followed by a list of requirements for that office. He concluded by saying, "He must have a firm grasp of the unchanging message of the tradition, so that he can be counted on for both expounding the sound doctrine and refuting those who argue against it" (Titus 1:9). The elder was the one being authorized to preside over the local church.

Church discipline is both possible and necessary where there is a clear succession of authority to authenticate. There are examples in Scripture where instructions and demands had to be made to correct improper or immoral behavior such as Paul encountered in Corinth. He had received reports of dissention and cliques disturbing the unity of the local congregation (1 Corinthians 1:10), and he admonished them to make up and be united in belief and practice. He'd also heard report of sexual immorality in the Corinthian church, and he gave instruction for discipline (1 Corinthians 5:1–5). The teaching of truth, and the behavior that goes with it, needed to be discerned and preserved. Even the authority of authentication does need some teeth in order to preserve what is being authenticated.

Throughout subsequent centuries, the authentication of the original faith was of prime importance. When serious controversies arose about doctrine, the great Ecumenical Councils of the Church, such as Nicaea in 325, Constantinople in 381, and Chalcedon in 451, were called to deal with them. Some modern authors, with a degree of prejudice, accuse these councils of inventing new doctrines. The situation is quite the opposite. The councils served to reduce ambiguity about what was already part of the deposit of faith. They firmed up the borders of what was consistent with apostolic teaching and excluded what was not consistent with it.

The whole Church, East and West, supported the proclamations of all these councils.

Sin in the House

Over the centuries, the authority system of the Church generally worked well for preserving doctrine and worship. Yet, although the ancient faith and tradition and liturgy had been well maintained, these were challenged by the sixteenth-century Reformers in the heat of the worldview shift of humanism. They justified their challenges by making charges of immorality and corruption against individual bishops. These leaders were indeed part of fallen humanity, and the virtue of holding office as bishop or pope did not prevent them from sinning. Today, Protestant critics of the Catholic Church still focus on the sins of those bishops and others who succumbed to the temptations of the cultural sophistication of the Renaissance. But this misses as an important truth: such individuals, though living in sin, never made any changes to the tradition or the teaching of the Church. Rather, they conveniently ignored them. It is not logical to blame doctrine and tradition that was ignored for an individual's choice to sin.

In Rome at the beginning of the sixteenth century, public morality was probably similar to that of Corinth fifteen hundred years earlier. The leadership of the Church at this time was not performing up to the standards of its doctrine and teaching. Remember, it was the personal behavior choices of the incumbents in office that caused their immorality and corruption.

Without question, changes were needed to remedy the situation if the Church was to be the salt and light to which it is called. But the real need was for the prelates in question to take the faith seriously, repent, and make personal life changes. It's illogical to blame apostolic tradition, liturgy, or Church teaching for the choices of these leaders to sin.

Dealing with sinning leaders has always presented a dilemma for the Church. To let the punishment fit the crime appeals to our cultural sense of justice. To severely punish the sinning leader would seem a reasonable course. However, even in the Old Testament, there is an example of a different spirit concerning Saul and David. Saul was seeking to kill David. On an expedition to find him, Saul entered a cave to use for a latrine. Unbeknownst to him, David and his men were hiding in the dark in that same cave. Instead of using the opportunity to kill Saul, David secretly cut off a piece of Saul's garment without being noticed. After Saul left, David then let the king know that though he'd had the opportunity, he could not kill "the Lord's anointed." This was in spite of Saul having become unworthy (1 Samuel 24:11–12). Although David himself had previously been anointed for kingship, yet he respected that Saul was still king under authority. David's time was yet to come.

Jesus said something controversial about a situation akin to the Renaissance-infused Church. Talking to a crowd as well as the disciples, he said, "The Scribes and the Pharisees occupy the chair of Moses. You must therefore do what they tell you and listen to what they say; but do not be guided by what they do" (Matthew 23:2–3). We hear lots of warnings against the Pharisees in their friction with Jesus' teaching, so it might surprise us that he didn't say to ignore them. In respect to their occupying the "chair of Moses," their authority regarding their doctrine still applied, and he said it must be obeyed. The Pharisees had the correct theology even if they did not live up to it. Might Jesus have possibly said the same thing about the "chair of Peter" in the sixteenth century?

Biblical Authority?

In their enthusiasm for the Reformation, most Protestants claim that authority stems not from a church but from the Scriptures themselves, especially the New Testament. Yet in claiming this, they fail to recognize that the apostolic succession of bishops and the tradition of the apostles were the authority that determined which books were to form the New Testament in the first place! Does the rejection of that authority by the Protestant Reformation cast some doubt on the validity of the choices those bishops made in closing the canon of Scripture? Martin Luther considered it—note his charge that the epistle of James was "an Epistle of Straw."[7] He wrote this remark in his preface to the New Testament, which he had translated.

Protestants should want to fully understand what the Reformers were protesting against—particularly so because the Church prior to the Reformation kept a unity close to that of John 17, but afterward exploded to the 30,000+ denominations in the last five hundred years. What were the Reformers protesting? We need to identify the sources of disunity in order to take our situation seriously. Were they protesting against the right things? In their zeal, did they wrongfully reject some means of grace and strength which had no connection even to sinning churchmen?

It was obvious reforms were needed, and different Reformers proceeded with changes they were convinced were necessary. Because of different educational viewpoints, however, the result was not one but three distinct reformations: the Catholic Reformation, the Protestant Reformation, and the Radical Reformation. We will look at each of them in turn. Before we do, however, it will benefit us to explore the key points of Catholicism—the heartbeat of the Ancient Church.

CHAPTER 6

UNDERSTANDING THE ANCIENT CHURCH

The Church founded in apostolic times remained virtually intact for a thousand years. In 1054 it split into an Eastern and Western branch, both of which continue intact to the present. We know them as the Orthodox and the Catholic Church. Technically these are not denominations but rather are the original Church. Together they account for over 70 percent of the world's Christians.

Christian denominations are the result of the Protestant Reformation, which made significant changes in ministry, authority structure, and sacraments from the first fifteen hundred years of Church tradition that preceded them. Those who have grown up in the denominations likely find the Catholic Church unfamiliar and somewhat mysterious. In this chapter, outlining some of the basic essentials of the Catholic Church (which generally also apply to the Orthodox Church) will hopefully clarify what might otherwise be a complex mystery. A clearer understanding of the essentials of the Catholic Church will also give us a clearer framework for understanding the Reformation.

The Church began with the infilling of the Holy Spirit as recorded in Acts 2. According to Acts 2:42, life in the Jerusalem Church continued with:

- The teaching of the apostles (their "tradition," or in the KJV, "doctrine")
- The brotherhood (in the KJV, "fellowship")
- The breaking of bread
- The prayers

The evangelical author Charles Swindoll refers to these as "the four essentials"[1] which are necessary for being a true Church. They were there at the beginning of the Church and continue in it today. Let's have a brief look at just what each one entailed.

Teaching (Doctrine). This was the content of what the apostles taught. It was their "tradition," their experiences of Jesus which they passed on in teaching the faithful and in evangelizing. This teaching was all oral tradition.

Brotherhood (Fellowship). This term may be somewhat ambiguous, but it is more than just general socializing. The Greek word for it is *koinonia,* which is literally translated "fellowship" or "partnership." It has the sense of the apostles working together in the common partnership of ministry, with a genuine unity. They were the ones in authority. They exercised it when they elected Matthias to replace Judas (Acts 1:26) and in establishing the order of deacons (Acts 6:1–5), as well as in teaching and governing the community.

Breaking of Bread. Reading through Acts and 1 Corinthians, we see that this term refers to the Lord's Supper. From the very beginning of the Church, it comprised a regular part of the worship on the first day of the week (Acts 20:7), being the day of Resurrection. It was a uniquely Christian rite and so took place in the people's houses instead of the temple or synagogue (Acts 2:46). Within very few decades it was called "Eucharist," the Greek term for thanksgiving.

The Prayers. The specificity of this term is clarified as we read on to Acts 3:1, where we are told of Peter and John going to the temple for "the prayers" at 3:00 p.m. The Jerusalem Church went to the temple to participate in its daily liturgical worship. The inclusion of "the prayers" is indicative that the earliest Church in Jerusalem would likely have used liturgical prayer in worship.

There are four key areas to explore in order to help understand the Catholic Church. These are: 1) the ministry, 2) the sacraments, 3) the creeds, and 4) the Bible. These areas are where there are differences between the Reformers and the Catholic Church.

In chapter 3 we examined in detail the origin of the ministry of bishops, priests, and deacons as found in Scripture and the post-apostolic era. In the Catholic Church, modern bishops are considered "true and authentic teachers of the faith."[2] They are the authorities who guarantee the authenticity of the teaching and tradition of the Church. The priest is ordained by the bishop and is considered "a co-worker of the Episcopal order."[3] The deacon is likewise ordained with the laying on of hands. The Orthodox Church follows this general pattern as well, but they do not have an international pope.

The Catholic Church recognizes the Bishop of Rome as Peter's successor and international archbishop over all Catholics. Peter is reputed to have been the first occupier of that position, hence we refer to it as the "Chair of Peter." As a bishop, the pope is not a dictator, nor does he create doctrine or invent theology. He authenticates the teachings of the Church to be what the apostles handed down and affirms and articulates the doctrine of the Church.

The Sacraments. Sacraments, or what you might call "sacred actions," may be controversial for some and unfamiliar or confusing to others. Most modern independent denominations do not recognize sacraments as such, but they may instead have two "ordinances," baptism and the Lord's Supper, because they were "ordered" by Jesus. Mainline Protestant Churches generally recognize these two but usually call them sacraments. There are significant differences between their interpretations of these actions and Catholic doctrine concerning them.

Though over time there was variability in the number of specified sacred actions in the Church, the seven sacraments which are alluded to in the Bible were the ones officially fixed in number by the Church in 1439.[4]

The Catholic and Orthodox Churches understand sacraments to be a point of connection between the physical and the spiritual and between the temporal and eternal. The old catechism defines a sacrament as "an outward and visible sign of an inward and spiritual grace."[5] The Catholic Catechism says, "The seven sacraments are the signs and instruments by which the Holy Spirit spreads the grace of Christ the head throughout the Church which is his Body."[6] In the Orthodox Church, they are also known as the "Holy Mysteries."

The seven sacraments are listed below. The commentary on each will include the associated scriptural references.

- Baptism
- Eucharist
- Confirmation

- Marriage
- Holy Orders
- Reconciliation
- Holy Unction

We need to point out that ritual is a valuable component of the administration of each of these. There is a principle in human nature that a special celebration is needed for us to fully connect with important events. Formality of ritual, including dressing appropriately, emphasizes the solemnity and importance of the occasion.

Baptism

There are three distinct entities in the New Testament under the name of baptism. The first was pre-Christian, done by John the Baptist. It was a baptism of repentance using water, but it was not done in the name of the Trinity. People frequently confuse this "water baptism" with the Christian sacrament of baptism "in the name of the Father, and of the Son, and of the Holy Spirit" (Matthew 28:19). Christian baptism is also done with water but is intended to make the person a member of the Body of Christ. This is the second baptism mentioned in Scripture.

Catholics and Orthodox do baptize adults, but they normally practice infant baptism. This has a Jewish precedent, where initiation into the Jewish faith was by circumcision of boys at eight days of age. They were not made to wait till they were much older, as would an adult convert, to decide to accept the Jewish faith and then be circumcised. Circumcision marks initiation into Judaism; likewise, baptism is the initiating sacrament into Christianity.

The third baptism, described in Acts, is often called the baptism of the Holy Spirit. The term has become somewhat more familiar after the Pentecostal revival of 1906. We will discuss this when we consider the sacrament of Confirmation.

The Christian sacrament of baptism is what Jesus commanded in the Great Commission, and it is administered in the name of the Trinity as commanded in Matthew 28:19. Its importance is emphasized by John, who quotes Jesus talking to Nicodemus: "Unless a man is born through water and the Spirit, he cannot enter the kingdom of God" (John 3:5). Next he said, You must be born from above" (John 3:7). The Greek word here is *anothen,* which literally means "from above"; the KJV translates it as "again." The essential features of Christian baptism are the Name, the water, and the Spirit.

Paul wrote to the Ephesians about baptism, describing the Church as follows: "He made her clean by washing her in water with a form of words" (Ephesians 5:26). He also wrote to Titus, "it was for no reason except his own compassion that he saved us, by means of the cleansing water of rebirth and by renewing us with the Holy Spirit" (Titus 3:5). Peter also wrote about baptism, after recounting the story of Noah's ark: "*that water* [which floated the ark] *is a type* [a foreshadowing] *of the baptism that saves you now*" (1 Peter 3:21).

These verses indicate that a grace, which is efficacious, is imparted in baptism. It has been maintained as such by the Catholic, Orthodox, and Anglican Church, as a once-in-a-lifetime event. Once you are a member of the family, you don't have to rejoin it.

The Eucharist (also named "the Mass")

This sacrament was instituted by Jesus at the Passover seder (supper) on the night he was betrayed (Matthew 26:26–29). The Passover celebrated God's power to save his people by looking back to the miracles of the Exodus that saved them from extinction and established them as a nation. Bread and wine were an integral part of this meal. Using the set prayers of blessing, Jesus would have followed this ritual with the bread, but he added the words "this is my body" before they took it to eat. Afterward, he likewise blessed the fourth cup of wine, the Elijah cup of the Seder ritual, in a similar manner, and added "this is my blood." They were all to drink of it.

Almost all Protestant denominations believe that Jesus was speaking metaphorically regarding the words "body" and "blood." The Reformers' contemporary, sixteenth-century worldview would not allow them to think otherwise. However, when we examine Scripture and the Christian writings of the period shortly after the apostles, we find there was a different worldview, and we see evidence that the Early Church took this more literally.

Paul wrote to the Corinthians, "The blessing-cup that we bless is a communion with the blood of Christ, and the bread that we break is a communion with the body of Christ. The fact that there is only one loaf means that, though there are many of us, we form a single body because we all have a share in this one loaf." Furthermore, he warned, "Everyone is to recollect himself before eating this bread and drinking this cup; because a person who eats and drinks without recognizing the [Lord's] Body is eating and drinking his own condemnation. In fact that is why many of you are weak and ill and some of you have died" (1 Corinthians 11:28–30). Such a severe consequence is most likely a result of desecration of the Lord's Body, rather than forgetting to think about the Last Supper.

Justin Martyr wrote describing the Eucharist about 155 AD, only about fifty years after the apostle John had died. He concluded by saying that the blessed bread and wine were not considered as common bread and wine, but rather the Lord's body and blood.[7] The gospel of John also has a long discourse by Jesus on the need to eat his body and drink his blood, after which many of his disciples left following him (John 6:56–66). These passages indicate a very early date for believing in the corporeal "Real Presence" of the Lord in the Eucharist. It was definitely not a later invention.

The Real Presence has been described by the Church as "transubstantiation," following Scholastic philosophy which considered reality to include both *substance* and *accidence*. Accidence is the visible and tactile aspect, sort of something's physics and chemistry. Substance is the underlying reality, which is changed when the bread and wine are blessed. In the eleventh century, transubstantiation was a new name to express in contemporary terms what the Church had believed from the beginning.

The purpose of receiving communion at the Eucharist is the regular nourishment of the Church's relationship with Jesus at least weekly, and on special days as well. The intention is to bring his presence freshly and regularly into ourselves in a tangible manner so that we can grow to be more like him. At the same time, it is a corporate action of the community as the family of God. "We all share in this one loaf."

Confirmation

Just before his ascension Jesus told the apostles to stay in Jerusalem to be baptized with the Holy Spirit (Acts 1:4–5). About fifty days after Passover, it happened: wind, fire, tongues, and new boldness of preaching by Peter. These gifts were not for the leaders alone, but for all members of the Church as the prophet Joel had foretold four hundred years earlier (Joel 2:28–32). Further in Acts, we read that after the Samaritans had been evangelized and baptized, Peter and John went there: "Then they laid hands on them and they received the Holy Spirit" (Acts 8:16). Early on, this practice accompanied baptism. In the East, instead of the bishop laying on hands, this is accomplished by use of Chrism, fragrant oil blessed by the bishop and applied by the priest at the time of baptism.

In the Western Church since about the fourth century, after infants were baptized, the bishop himself normally did the laying on of hands at what is called the sacrament of Confirmation. This sacrament was administered some time later, when the baptized child was older and had been instructed. The Catechism states, "It is evident from its celebration that the effect of the sacrament of Confirmation is the full outpouring of the Holy Spirit as once granted to the apostles on the day of Pentecost."[8]

Some Protestant Churches have "confirmation," but it normally is to allow those baptized in infancy to take on their baptismal vows for themselves. This is obviously of a different intention from the sacrament in the Catholic Church.

Protestant Reformers generally believed that the "sign gifts" of the Holy Spirit ceased with the death of the apostles. It took the 1906 Azusa Street revival in California to bring a return of "Pentecostalism," which emphasized the baptism of the Holy Spirit with all the gifts of the Spirit as listed in 1 Corinthians 12. The Catechism, in the quote above, would make it appear that all Catholics should be charismatic, since all are expected to become confirmed.

Marriage

Marriage and procreation are God's invention. In Genesis we read that he created man, male and female, in his own image and told them to multiply, fill the earth, and conquer it.

Then he said this creation was "very good" (Genesis 1:27–31). Jesus was at a wedding in Cana, and for his first miracle, he provided the wine (John 2:1–10). Later, when the Pharisees questioned him about divorce, Jesus answered, "This is why a man must leave father and mother, and cling to his wife, and the two become one body . . . So then, what God has united, man must not divide" (Matthew 19:5–6). Jesus was declaring that marriage is a lifelong union of one man and one woman, united by God. In essence, this is a covenant relationship between the couple and God.

The Catechism states, "Christian marriage in its turn becomes an efficacious sign, the sacrament of the covenant of Christ and the Church. Since it signifies and communicates grace, marriage between baptized persons is a true sacrament of the New Covenant."[9] It is something holy, and not simply a civil contract.

In the history of Jewish culture, fecundity is a blessing and barrenness a curse. Sex is good; it is God's invention. It is meant to be a blessing and to increase his kingdom. The ascetic virtue of virginity can carry a risk of resembling the concept in Greek culture and lore. Greek philosophy touts the dualism of the "physical" being evil and only the "spirit" being good and having value. In Jewish culture, to have many children is considered a blessing from the Lord.

Holy Orders

God is a God of order as well as the source of authority. The sacrament of Holy Orders is the means by which a person receives the impartation of the authority to minister and to celebrate sacraments. It is conferred by the laying on of hands by bishops. Paul made explicit reference to this in writing to Timothy, who was to read to the people and preach and teach.

"You have a spiritual gift which was given to you when the prophets spoke and the body of elders laid their hands on you" (1 Timothy 4:14).

The Catholic Church has maintained this tradition for nearly two thousand years, as have the Orthodox. A single bishop may ordain priests and deacons, though the consecration of a bishop requires a minimum of three bishops to accomplish it. The formal sacrament of ordination, or Holy Orders, helps ensure a reliable means of guarding and passing on the faith. If people were to take it upon themselves to do ministry, where would the guarantee of their authenticity come from? It would risk being a "going" without being sent. The purpose of Holy Orders is the impartation of the authority and authorization, extending from the apostles, to minister the sacraments and authenticate and communicate the gospel message.

Reconciliation

This is the sacrament of absolving from sin. It is pronounced by a bishop or priest on the authority imparted by Jesus after his Resurrection, when he said, "Receive the Holy Spirit. For those whose sins you forgive, they are forgiven; for those sins you retain, they are retained" (John 20:22–23). By this, he authorized the apostles, and by implication their successors, to have this function.

The penitent confesses his sins and must be fully repentant. The purpose is to reconcile the person to return to fellowship with God and with the Church. Early on, the rigorous public discipline of penance was required before absolution and restoration were granted. This meant confessing your sins to the whole congregation. In the seventh century, Irish monks with Eastern mystical influence introduced private confession and penance.[10]

Holy Unction

Unction here refers to anointing with oil for the purpose of healing the sick. The customary postponement until the deathbed has given it the name of "Last Rites." Its purpose is found in the epistle of James: "If one of you is ill, he should send for the elders of the church, and they must anoint him with oil in the name of the Lord, and pray over him. The prayer of faith will save the sick man and the Lord will raise him up again; and if he has committed any sins, they will be forgiven" (James 5:14–15). The wording of Scripture here implies that healing and forgiveness of sins are the primary intention.

The Creeds and the Scriptures

We have now completed some basic familiarization with the areas where the Protestant Reformers took the most issue concerning the 1500-year-old Church that preceded them. The creeds and Scriptures also came under some criticism by different Reformers in their battle with the Catholic Church.

The Creeds

The purpose of the creeds is to defend the faith from drift and innovation. Generally, the mainline denominations received them with minor adjustments, such as replacing the word "Catholic" with the word "Christian." Though the Apostles Creed is accepted by many Protestants, the words "communion of saints" are not taken seriously or discussed, despite being recited. There is a variety of attitudes among the more Radical Reformers on the topic of creeds, and some make an accusation of "creedalism."

Most of the youth from many denominations today are unfamiliar with the creeds. Below, we are quoting both the Apostles Creed and the Nicene Creed as used presently in the

Catholic Church. It may be useful to reread chapter 3 to review the origin and dates of the creeds.

The Apostles Creed

I believe in God, the Father almighty, Creator of heaven and earth, and in Jesus Christ, his only Son, our Lord, who was conceived by the Holy Spirit, born of the Virgin Mary, suffered under Pontius Pilate, was crucified, died and was buried; he descended into hell; on the third day he rose again from the dead; he ascended into heaven, and is seated at the right hand of God the Father almighty; from there he will come to judge the living and the dead. I believe in the Holy Spirit, the holy catholic Church, the communion of saints, the forgiveness of sins, the resurrection of the body, and life everlasting. Amen.

[The roots of this creed date back to the first century AD.]

The Nicene Creed:

I believe in one God, the Father almighty, maker of heaven and earth, of all things visible and invisible. I believe in one Lord Jesus Christ, the Only Begotten Son of God, born of the Father before all ages. God from God, Light from Light, True God from true God, begotten not made, consubstantial with the Father; through him all things were made. For us men and for our salvation he came down from heaven, and by the Holy Spirit was incarnate of the Virgin Mary, and became man.

For our sake he was crucified under Pontius Pilate, he suffered death and was buried, and rose again on the third day in accordance with the Scriptures. He ascended into heaven and is seated at the right hand of the Father. He will come again in glory to judge the living and the dead and his kingdom will have no end.

I believe in the Holy Spirit, the Lord, the giver of life, who proceeds from the Father and the Son, who with the Father and the Son is adored and glorified, who has spoken through the prophets. I believe in one, holy catholic and apostolic Church. I confess one baptism for the forgiveness of sins and I look forward to the resurrection of the dead and the life of the world to come. Amen.

[Dates from 325 AD and 381 AD][11]

The Scriptures

We have already dealt with the use of the Septuagint as the basis for the Old Testament for the first fifteen hundred years of the Church. The Orthodox Church has forty-nine books in its Old Testament. The Catholic Bible has forty-six books. The Protestant Reformers felt compelled to remove the books they felt were not divinely inspired, thereby reducing the number to thirty-nine. There is, however, full agreement among all Christians as to the twenty-seven books of the New Testament.

The Four Marks

Within the Catholic Church, there are four "marks" that describe the doctrine about the Church as it is intended to be as the Body of Christ. These descriptive qualities are listed in the Nicene Creed, namely, the Church is:

- One
- Holy

- Catholic
- Apostolic

One. Jesus prayed for his Church to be one. Paul reminded us that "all of us, in union with Christ, form one body, and as parts of it we belong to each other" (Romans 12:5). For the Ancient Church, each congregation is a local manifestation of that one Church, sharing the same ministry and sacraments with all the rest of the whole Church. Catholic and Orthodox hold this view.

Holy. The Church is holy because it is indwelt by the Holy Spirit. Paul addressed the Corinthian Church as "the holy people of Jesus" (1 Corinthians 1:2). The Church depends on the power of the Holy Spirit, both for making the sacraments efficacious and for leading and empowering the laity (saints) and the clergy in exercising ministry, evangelism, and the life of the Church.

Catholic. This word comes from the Greek, and it means whole or complete. It refers to the whole faith believed by the apostles. It includes tradition and doctrine as well as ministry, sacraments, and Scripture. It is an ancient term in use in the Church from at least 108 AD.

Apostolic. This refers not only to the lineage of the apostles and their faith, but it also includes the mission of the Church as expressed in the Great Commission. Every member of the Church has responsibility to participate in the apostolic mission.

The Church Year

All Christians are familiar with celebrating Christmas and Easter. However, these are part of an area of church life in general that is not well known in Protestant circles. The Church Year utilizes every Sunday of the year to follow and celebrate the life of Jesus. Each grouping of Sundays is referred to as a season and is marked by the appropriate theme.

The seasons are:

Advent. A time of preparation for the Incarnation, or birth of Jesus, as well as for his Second Coming.

Christmas. Christ Mass celebrates Jesus' birth. It lasts twelve days, beginning with the Midnight Mass on Christmas Eve until Epiphany.

Epiphany. Celebrated January 6, this day draws its name from *epi phaneros,* Greek for the "showing forth" of Jesus to the Gentiles as seen in the coming of the wise men.

Lent. This is the season for spiritual "spring house cleaning." It involves prayer, fasting, and giving alms, as a discipline lasting forty days, to prepare for the Cross and our Lord's Resurrection. Sundays are not included in the forty days for fasting because they celebrate Jesus' Resurrection.

Easter. The celebration of the Resurrection. The season lasts till Ascension Day.

Pentecost. This holy day celebrates the birth of the Church with the infilling of the Holy Spirit in the Upper Room and for the whole Church.

Sundays in Ordinary Time. The Sundays outside a specified season.

We need to appreciate that the doctrine of the Church; its ministry of bishops, priests, and deacons; and the sacraments, creeds, and even the New Testament all came to be in place following from the tradition of the apostles passed down in the Church. Professor Andrew Fix claims that some devotional traditions have also come up from the laity, such as the Rosary and the Stations of the Cross.[12]

It is hoped that this brief survey of the Ancient Church will help us to understand what the Catholic Church is and where it came from. Notice that every rite, or sacrament, has a direct connection to our Lord's relationship with his body, the Church. We have attempted to give a clear and reasonably complete, yet simple, picture of the basics of the Catholic (and Orthodox) Church in order to better appreciate their relationship to the Protestant Reformation. As we look at the three reformations, it will be most valuable to understand where each side is coming from and what they mean by the terms they use.

CHAPTER 7

THE BEGINNING OF REFORM: THE CATHOLIC REFORMATION

In both phases of the Foggy Gap, we saw that despite the pressures and stresses that distracted and sometimes even infected the Church, multiple efforts were made from within to steer it back on course. In medieval times, the Church was weakened spiritually by carrying the added burden of civil government. Some leaders of the state as well as those of the Church recognized the need to correct the slippage of morals and laxity of religious instruction, and they made sporadic efforts to rectify the situation with some degree of success.

Originally, all of the efforts for reform had one aim: that of restoring the Church to live true to its teaching. This impetus for reform changed in nature, however, and during the sixteenth century it ripped at the heart of the Church, exploding into three divergent pathways.

The Catholic Reform was the earliest and lasted the longest. In one sense, provision for Catholic reform was there from the beginning. Recall that even in the New Testament, Paul had to write Corinth to admonish them for the immorality that had invaded their ranks and direct them to reform their behavior. A few centuries later, the Council of Nicaea had to deal with serious false teaching.

For many evangelicals, the term "Catholic Reformation" conjures up the more familiar term "Counter-Reformation," with Catholic reforms seen as a response to the loss of the Protestants in the sixteenth century. The reality is quite different. In general, that century began with European public morality in an abysmal state, and even clergy morals and competence were compromised. The faith was not adequately being taught, and preaching was rare or absent in churches. However, by the time of the Protestant Reformation, change was already well underway in the Catholic Church. A careful look will reveal a significant head-start of reform and revival in Spain a century earlier.

The Renaissance with its humanist philosophy had arrived later in Spain than in Italy, so its unsavory aspects of pagan immorality had less influence there. It may be partly because of this that the effort for reform began here far sooner than in the rest of Europe. Early in the fifteenth century, a Spanish Dominican monk named Vincent Ferrar (1350–1419)[1] was a gifted preacher who was highly educated in philosophy and theology, and had served with the Avignon papacy. Being ascetic, he turned down being made a cardinal, but did accept the papal assignment of a lengthy preaching mission in Spain. This is an example of the expected normal papal response to the need for reform. Vincent's mission emphasis dealt with sin, judgment, and repentance. He spent eight years in Spain, and his preaching even won thousands of Jews and Muslims to the faith. He personally attended to sick children and did many miracles of healing. He was canonized as a saint in 1455.

This saint wasn't doing reform in the sense understood by most Protestants. He did not reject any Church teaching, nor did he devise new practices or doctrines. Rather, he pointed the people back to the tradition of faith the apostles had taught by preaching the gospel! This was the kind of reform the Church was supposed to do continually.

Another gifted Spaniard was Ximenes de Cisneros (1436–1517), a well-educated priest who became confessor (spiritual mentor) to Queen Isabella in 1492 and Archbishop of Toledo in 1494.[2] He was a member of the conservative branch of the followers of Francis of Assisi, the "Observants," who worked to improve the morals and education of clergy. The result of this man's ministry was a marked revival of piety among the people of Spain.

Ximenes also founded the University of Alcala as a center for teaching the faith in Spain. He supported the production of a "polyglot Bible" with side-by-side translations in Latin, Greek, Hebrew, and Aramaic to aid study of Scripture. He also made use of the newly invented printing press. These efforts resulted in significant improvements in clergy training and morals as well as improving the spiritual life of the general populace.

By the fifteenth century, Islamic warriors had conquered much of Spain. The Spanish royal government used military force to defend themselves and reclaimed Grenada in 1482. Archbishop Talavera (1428–1507)[3] attempted to convert (or reconvert) the Muslim populace in Grenada by persuasion and tact. Thousands responded to his efforts and were baptized.[4] However, Ximenes in his zeal was less patient than Archbishop Talavera and succumbed to the temptation to utilize governmental coercion. King Ferdinand and his wife, Isabella, responded by providing full royal governmental backing.

This involved the Inquisition. Just the mention of this topic conjures up gruesome images of cruel punishments and burning at the stake. It is too easy to forget that similar practices were used by Mainline Protestant Reformers in their dealing with Anabaptist Protestants. Such use of force was a sign of the times. To love your enemies was unpopular, the end was considered to justify the means. After all, the thinking was that since they were heretics leading others to hell, such treatment was therefore justified.

The use of such un-Christian methods of enforcement, illustrates just how deeply the Church had been invaded by worldliness of the culture during the feudal era. The Church was just blindly following the normal, accepted pattern of the day. Protestants later did likewise. It was the government that administered the actual punishments through chosen inquisitors such as Torquemada.

Despite their "zeal for the faith," Isabella, Ximenes, and Torquemada were never "sainted," their methodology being totally inconsistent with the faith.[5] The Church just could not bless such un-Christian behavior, no matter what the cause.

The Situation in Italy

The efforts for Catholic reform began later in Italy and were less organized than was the case in Spain. This was probably because Italy was the epicenter of Renaissance humanism with its prominent acceptance of pagan immorality, and the sophisticated populace had accepted this corruption. Church hierarchy was largely in synch with the humanist thrust, making papal leadership for reform lacking. Enthusiasm for pagan art and literature, and patronage of humanist endeavors, captivated the prelates of the Church as much as the rest of the upper classes. Some even sponsored virtually pagan humanist teachers and artisans. Spiritual reform supported by the Vatican had to wait till Paul III (1534–1549) was made pope.[6]

In 1497, there was a small beginning of reform in Rome with the formation of a small group called the Oratory of Divine Love, whose emphasis was moral reform within the Church. Giovanni P Caraffa (1476–1559) was a prominent member who ministered by visiting hospitals and prisons.[7] He was the founder of a second group called the Theatines, who promoted clergy reform and renewal. He later became Pope Paul IV.

In 1530, the Regular Clerics of St. Paul was formed. This group was closely associated with the parish church of St. Barnabas in Milan. Their aim was to teach the faith, to hear confessions, to conduct missions, and to revive a "zeal for souls" among clergy.[8]

A particularly remarkable Catholic reformer and evangelist before 1500 was Giralamo Savonarola (1452–1498).[9] He rejected the Renaissance values and corruption that had infected society and the Church. Savonarola became a Dominican monk, and in 1481 he moved to the monastery at San Marko in Florence. At the time, Florence was the hotbed of Renaissance culture. Savonarola was a highly educated and gifted preacher who proclaimed God's judgment on the vulgar culture and sins of the populace. He urged Florence and all Italy to "repent and return to Christ." They responded with a major revival. Churches became crowded, and lives changed remarkably.[10]

During Lent in 1497, Savonarola's preaching changed the annual Carnival, a festival similar to the modern Mardi Gras in New Orleans. The masks, indecent pictures, books, and other paraphernalia associated with the yearly celebration were collected and burned in a huge bonfire.

Unfortunately, the cleansing of Carnival and the revival were short lived because of civil politics. It had taken place prior to the unification of Italy. Florence was still an independent republic at the time of revival, and the following year, 1498, the city allied itself with France instead of Italy. This enraged the pope, Alexander VI (from the notorious Borgia family), who then turned his anger on Savonarola for purely political, and not religious reasons.[11] Savonarola was excommunicated and executed. After this, Florence gradually slipped back into its old ways. However, a few lives did remain changed, including the artists Botticelli and Michelangelo and the Christian humanist Pico della Mirandola.[12] Though he was executed before 1500, Savonarola planted seeds of Catholic reform in those who continued in the wake of his influence.

The Society of Jesus

Another Catholic reformer of Spanish origin who came into prominence later was Ignatius Loyola (1491–1556). He started out as a soldier, and while recovering from war wounds had a conversion experience. As a result, he wrote a document called *Spiritual Exercises* for the examination of conscience. He afterward studied at the University of Alcala and the University of Paris. He was spiritually devout and became highly educated, obtaining a Master of Arts degree in theology.[13]

Along with several devout University of Paris companions, Ignatius founded the Society of Jesus in 1534. Their original vision was to go to Jerusalem and convert the Muslims, but this never materialized. The Society was officially authorized by the pope in 1540.[14] The basic aim of the "Jesuits," as they were called, was to work "for the good of souls" and the propagation of the faith wherever they should be sent. Along with teaching children and adults, public preaching, and expounding Scripture, they also did charitable works. They were intensely disciplined and, in the chain of authority, were directly responsible to the pope, and they labored for moral reform. Their special emphasis was the education of youth to produce moral character. Still in existence today, they have effectively evangelized many of the far-flung places around the world.

The End of the Renaissance Papacy

The worldliness of the Renaissance papacy came to an end with the ascension of Alexander Farnese to the chair of Peter as Paul III (1534–1549).[15] He was a reformer at heart and proposed to begin with the cardinals of the Curia. He commenced by appointing worthy men from multiple countries as new cardinals and then organized a committee to do a *Report of Cardinals and other Prelates of the Church,* addressing abuses in morals, doctrine, and other areas. In 1537 they reported their assessment of the state of the Church,[16] having identified twenty-six areas needing reform.

Paul III believed that the necessary organizational reforms were so major that a general council was in order. Politics precluded meeting in major cities in Italy or Germany, so Trent, a fortified city in northern Italy, was finally the agreed site. Lutherans were invited, but Luther responded with a document, "Against the Roman Papacy Founded by the Devil."[17] The council began without them in 1545 and continued to hold meetings until it was suspended in 1547 because of an outbreak of the plague and political complications. Paul died in 1549.

Like the previous Church councils, the aim of the Council of Trent was not to create new doctrine but rather to "seek the common mind of the Church"[18] and clarify, among the variety of viewpoints in existence, which ones agreed with apostolic teaching. Pope Julius III (1550–1555) continued to carry out the reform efforts and recommendations of the council, including revising papal election regulations. He reconvened the Council of Trent May 1551–April 1552, and among other concerns, they dealt with questions of penance and Eucharistic doctrine.[19] Later, the Council of Trent reconvened from 1562–1563. This session dealt with discipline, dogma, and response to the Protestant doctrinal changes.[20]

The Catholic Reformation has often been called the "Counter-Reformation" by Protestant historians, but as we see, it was more complicated than that. We have noted that the Catholic reform movement had already begun near the year 1400, and reform efforts had continued with varying degrees of effectiveness, culminating in the Council of Trent. The Renaissance license of loose living among clergy, from the top down, was curtailed. Nepotism, political control of the Church, and Church finances had all come under scrutiny and been corrected, and the quality of spirituality within the Church was markedly improved.

The Council of Trent reaffirmed the doctrine and the authority structure of the Church as it had been from apostolic times. The Vulgate was affirmed as the authorized Bible, and the injunction of Peter in 2 Peter 1:20 against private scriptural interpretation was retained.[21] The efficacy of infant baptism was also reaffirmed, as was justification by both faith and grace. The doctrine of "free will" was stated as man's ability to cooperate with or to reject grace.

The seven sacraments (Baptism, Confirmation, Eucharist, Marriage, Holy Orders, Reconciliation, and Holy Unction) were reaffirmed. They were to be performed only by authorized clergy, who were the shepherds of the flock, and not by laymen as advocated in the new doctrine of many Protestant denominations.[22]

In the Eucharist, the doctrine of transubstantiation was maintained and reaffirmed the corporeal Real Presence of the body and blood of Jesus when the bread and wine are consecrated. (Luther was the only Protestant Reformer to retain a similar doctrine.) The concept was not new. It was alluded to by Paul (1 Corinthians 11:28–31) and stated by Justin Martyr in 155 AD, and it was (and is) accepted by both the Orthodox and

Catholic Churches. Trent also reasoned that since the totality of Jesus was present in either the consecrated bread or wine, the chalice was not mandatory and could be dispensed with for the laity. It has been restored to the laity in many places in modern times.

By the end of the Council of Trent in1563, the Catholic Church had been cleansed of the major abuses that had challenged it over several centuries. The doctrine, practices, and organizational structure of ancient times were reaffirmed. Kenneth Latourette points out that the effect of the Protestant Reformation on the Council of Trent was to decrease the degree of the permitted diversity of doctrinal viewpoints allowable in the Catholic Church.[23] This is because when a doctrine is not challenged, some ambiguity about it can be tolerated. However, when it is challenged or attacked, precision is needed to define the boundaries of its exact meaning.

Trent did define, with more precision, the perceived apostolic understanding of numerous doctrines and eliminated the previous allowed diversity. Its whole aim was to maintain the faith as originally intended and taught from the time of the Early Church and to reject the promulgation of new doctrines. The Council of Trent perceived the Protestant Reformation to have proposed many questionable new doctrines.

CHAPTER 8

THE PROTESTANT REFORMATION

What became the Protestant Reformation began as part of the Catholic movement to cleanse the Church from moral and political behavior resulting from medieval conflicts of interest and rising Renaissance humanism. As we have already seen, efforts at reform had already been exercised for over a century with some encouraging results. But the early sixteenth century was a time of profound intellectual ferment, driven by Renaissance humanism, which provided a climate ripe for change. New and radical ideas were just waiting to be triggered into action. What became the Protestant stream of reform was now ready to utilize some of these new ideas and diverge into its own distinct and separate path.[1]

As always, there is more to the story than can be seen on the surface. Latourette points out that the reformers who remained Catholic generally tended to come from the nobility, and those who eventually left the Catholic Church generally came from the peasantry, no matter how highly educated they became.[2] Undoubtedly those from the nobility were more committed to the prevailing authority structure and therefore more patient with making changes. Conversely, those from the peasantry might have felt abused by the upper classes, and this may have predisposed them to demand more rapid results from their reform efforts.

Our own twenty-first-century education emphasizes the intellectual and artistic benefits of the Renaissance but soft peddles the anti-spiritual dimensions of the human self-sufficiency and spirit of independence that preferred to ignore God and morality.[3] Henry Lucas lists several precipitators that helped induce the Protestant Reformation. These include the clash of Church authority and rising European nationalism along with the growth of commerce and the mercantile class in the cities, who then had the free time to pursue education in Greek philosophy and arts. This new bourgeoisie often attained an educational level that equaled or surpassed that of the clergy, and along with it, they developed an eagerness for change.[4] It was into this milieu that Reformers' ideas entered the scene. Three major Reformers emerged, and their teaching resulted in their departure from the Catholic Church and the eventual formation of mainline Protestant denominations.

The Three Major Reformers: Luther, Zwingli, and Calvin

The First Reformer: Luther

The iconic figure who catalyzed the Protestant Reformation had his destiny ignited by a lightning bolt. The young Martin Luther had just finished his master's degree at Erfurt University and begun the study of law.[5] Walking home one stormy night in Germany, a bolt of lightning struck near him, knocking him to the ground. To his surprise, he did not die. Shaken up, he realized that God had spared his life, and consequently he felt obliged to become a monk—the natural response to such a miracle in those days. By this decision, his parents' hopes for a lawyer son were dashed. Had it not been for that lightning bolt, we would never have known the name of Martin Luther. He would have been just another obscure medieval lawyer.

In his new life as a monk, Luther studied theology and within two years was ordained as a priest.[6] He suffered a great deal of anguish of soul over the awareness of his own sinfulness and his inability to experience a sense of certainty of salvation.[7] This was probably exacerbated by the ascetic emphasis of that day and by the intensity of his study of St Augustine on the nature of sin, original sin, and predestination. Since his youth, he had been afraid of God and afraid of Jesus as judge, which was likewise not uncommon for the spirituality of the time. This left him preoccupied with finding assurance of salvation. Despite this, he went on to earn a doctorate of theology and was assigned the duty of lecturing to those studying to become priests.[8]

While meditating, in preparation to teach on Paul's epistle to the Romans, Luther had a sudden experience of enlightenment as he read the words, "The just shall live by faith" (Romans 1:17). These words brought instant relief as it occurred to him that instead of trying to earn God's favor, he needed only have faith in what Jesus did on the cross, to be justified before God.[9] He was so impressed by this that he felt the need to add the word "alone" to what the verse in Romans says. Thus began the doctrine of *Sola Fide* (faith alone), which became the rallying cry of the ensuing Protestant Reformation.

Luther read the whole Bible in the light of this concept and subsequently questioned several New Testament books as lacking support for "faith alone." At first he felt they should be removed from the Bible, referring to the epistle of James as "the epistle of straw" because of its emphasis on good works. He eventually did accept the whole New Testament as divinely inspired and genuine.

He continued in his position of teaching seminary students for probably another five years. This normal life was rudely interrupted in 1517 as a result of a papal proclamation of an indulgence to benefit the construction of St. Peter's in Rome and raise finances for the archbishop of Mainz.[10] To Protestants, what an indulgence consists of is a foreign concept. It is not a license to sin, but rather, as Lucas puts it, "An indulgence was simply the remission of the penalty imposed for a sin already forgiven."[11] Sin was understood to have two parts, guilt and the temporal penalty that was imposed after the guilt was repented and forgiven. Technically indulgences were not to be sold but true repentance was required and a free will offering could be given. The poor were not required to pay any money. However, John Tetzel, a Dominican monk, was enthusiastically hawking 'the sale' of these indulgences in Germany in a manner well beyond the authorized process. Tetzel was famous for his legendary sales pitch "when the coin in the coffer rings, the soul from purgatory springs."

It should be noted that the intention of purgatory is the provision for completion of sanctification of the deceased who is already bound for heaven (i.e. "the saved"), to be ready to participate in heavenly life. Tales of the process are often fuel for speculation.

Luther was appalled at this abuse by Tetzel and preached against it. He wanted to encourage discussion at the academic level within the Church regarding his concerns about indulgences and their abuse, as well as questioning their validity. He advertised this proposal in the manner normal for the day by posting his ninety-five topics (theses) for discussion on the castle church door at Wittenberg on October 31, 1517.[12] But instead of inspiring a university debate as he intended, his theses were circulated widely in German as well as in Latin by his sympathizers, who used the printing press to do it. These questions concerning indulgences, the Church, and

Church politics struck a chord with the German population in general.

As a result of the variety of circulating public opinions on these topics, the pope called Luther to Rome in 1518 to face heresy charges. The venue was, mercifully for Luther, changed to a more favorable Germany, at Augsburg, to a meeting called a "Diet." Although Luther was challenged, the outcome was that John Tetzel was censured for his method of indulgence hawking.[13] Nevertheless, this meeting marked the beginning of the unstoppable course of the Protestant Reformation. Luther was a dynamic leader whose writings and action inspired others to seriously pursue the reforms he advocated. The scene was about to undergo a massive transition.

During 1520, defending his position, Luther published five passionate tracts. In particular, these expressed his developing complaints against the Catholic Church, both doctrinal and practical. They included "Sermon on Good Works," "The Papacy at Rome," "An Address to the German Nobility," "The Babylonian Captivity of the Church," and "Freedom of the Christian Man."[14] These were all, in effect, polemics against the Catholic Church. Through continued teaching, writing, and refuting of his critics, Luther's ideas and position were becoming more solidified.

What followed is not exactly an example of civil discourse. Rather than assuring that each side fully understood exactly what the other meant by each idea and then discussing it in a calm, academic manner, Luther and the Catholic hierarchy both dug in their heels and hardened their positions. Luther was a man of passion, and when challenged he could be aggressive and overly assertive.[15]

Soon, Luther began to reject the ultimate right of the Church to interpret Scripture. For the previous fifteen hundred years, the episcopacy (bishops) and tradition of the Church had final responsibility for this function. In his tract "To the Christian Nobility of the German Nation," Luther said that because of the "priesthood of all believers," every true believer was competent to discern correctness in matters of faith, in referring to the interpretation of Scripture.[16]

Luther also challenged the "superiority" of the clergy over the laity with perhaps a sense that the clergy was exerting a tyranny over them. The "priesthood of all believers" concept would definitely suggest some relief. Perhaps this idea was reinforced by the first epistle of Peter: "But you are a chosen race, a royal priesthood, a consecrated nation, a people set apart to sing the praises of God" (1 Peter 2:9). However, this "priesthood" is rendered somewhat more metaphoric by what Peter says later in this epistle: "Now I have something to tell your elders . . . Be shepherds of the flock of God that is entrusted to you . . . Never be a dictator over any group that is put in your charge, but be an example the whole flock can follow" (1 Peter 5:1–3).

Peter does not give the sheep the same authority as the shepherd; rather the elder, as clergy, is to give servant leadership to the congregation in his charge. Yet Luther seemed to favor giving the sheep the same authority as the shepherds. He went so far as to consider that the sacrament of ordination was an "invention of the Church of Rome."[17] Luther supported further changes in doctrine by challenging transubstantiation in the Eucharist, despite holding a very similar view himself. He also rejected five of the seven sacraments, claiming they had no support in Scripture and implying they too were an invention of Rome.[18] This is probably an example of selective reading of Scripture that overlooks areas you don't agree with.

By January 1521, Luther's writing and teaching had earned him the sentence of excommunication.[19] In April of that year he was summoned to the Diet at Worms to recant and be restored to the Church or to defend his writings. He chose the latter, basing his defense on what he interpreted Scripture to say. He concluded with the famous words, "Here I stand."

Luther's defense was a profound, unambiguous public statement that Scripture was to be the sole final authority in matters of faith and doctrine. The Latin term used was *Sola Scriptura*, meaning "Bible alone," which became the second cry of the Protestant Reformation. It was eagerly embraced by all Protestant adherents. The acceptance of this proclamation eliminated two of the three strands of the authority structure of the Church: the direct authenticating continuity of the historical past, residing in the apostolic succession of the bishops, and the apostolic tradition that had been handed down.

Luther had not convinced his adversaries this time, and an edict was issued that forbade anyone to give him food, drink, or lodging and ordered his imprisonment. With so many German sympathizers, he was provided refuge in the castle at Wartburg for nearly a year. It was here he wrote a dozen books and translated the Bible into the German vernacular. Within a year, he returned to the university in Wittenberg and openly resumed leadership of the reform movement.[20]

During the year of Luther's absence, the reform movement had spread rapidly. There were widespread new divisions and new doctrines in the new church, with an atmosphere of impending chaos. Luther's response was in keeping with his view of the divinely ordered role of civil government. According to Latourette, he persuaded the German government to divide up the domain into districts, with a government "religious supervisor" for each one. These had authority over clergy and enforced uniformity of worship in the local church.[21]

In essence, this civil involvement marked the functioning emergence of the Lutheran Church.

Luther was the most conservative of the three major Reformers. He had a distaste for Renaissance humanism, so was less influenced by it than were the other two. He believed in using music in worship along with congregational singing. Though he did make doctrinal changes, including changes to the form of ministry in the Church and reducing the number of sacraments, his deviation from the Catholic Church was less dramatic that either Zwingli's or Calvin's. He allowed voluntary confession, the use of the crucifix, and candles and images on condition they were "not venerated."

The Second Reformer: Zwingli

Simultaneous with the Reformation in Germany, there was a Protestant reform movement in Switzerland. The leader here, Huldreich Zwingli (1484–1531), was originally a Catholic priest, trained at humanist universities in Basel, Berne, and Vienna. He had earned both bachelor's and master's degrees and was made pastor at Glarus in 1506.[22] In 1518 he ended up in Zurich. He enthusiastically endorsed Luther's writings, but he was more influenced by humanism than was Luther.[23]

Like Luther, Zwingli claimed to espouse Sola Scriptura as his source of doctrinal authority and his basis for judging the Catholic Church. Undoubtedly, humanism also played a major part in his thinking. He came to reject the validity of monastic vows, clerical celibacy, and the intercession of saints. Like many other priests of that era, he had not kept his clerical vow of celibacy, but in 1522 began to cohabit with a woman whom he finally married in 1524.[24]

By 1525, his radical austerity in religious ritual had progressed to the rejection of displaying images and relics and of the use of church organs. In fact, he opposed the use of any music in worship. As priest in charge, he discontinued the Mass in the church in Zurich as being "idolatrous," replacing it with a much simpler ceremony devoid of any hint of "sacrifice" or "superstitious practices" and allowing no music.[25] The idea was to omit anything not specifically ordained in the Bible. Zwingli retained only two sacraments, baptism and the Lord's Supper. (For him, baptism still included that of infants.)

An attempt to consolidate the Protestant reform movement was made by the main Reformers by calling a conference at Marburg Castle in October 1529. The leading Reformers—Bucer, Melanchthon, and Luther from Germany and Zwingli from Zurich—were in attendance. After several days of meeting, they issued the Fifteen Marburg Articles, voicing agreement on key areas of the faith[26] except for the doctrine of Real Presence at the Eucharist. Luther was firm that "is" meant "is" and not "represents." Zwingli staunchly maintained that the words "This is my body" were purely metaphoric, like when Jesus said "I am the vine" or "I am the door." Rather than unifying the Protestant Reformation as hoped, Marburg made the rupture between Reformers permanent. The two extremes on this one key issue were totally incompatible, making a separation of ways unavoidable.

Like Luther, Zwingli also respected the civil government as being divinely ordered, therefore insisting that all aspects of church discipline and religious order be conducted with full government cooperation. He gained control of the Zurich city council, which came to function as a veritable theocracy. Zwingli was a powerful preacher and won over many cantons (Swiss city-states), as well as making inroads into southern Germany. Relations of the Catholic cantons with Zurich became strained, worsening when Zurich imposed a food embargo on them. That action precipitated a military conflict. Zwingli took part in the action as chaplain of the Zurich troops and was killed in the battle at Kappel on October 11, 1531.[27]

The Third Reformer: Calvin

John Calvin (1509–1564) was born near Paris. He began as a student at the age of fourteen at the University of Paris.[28] He was keenly interested in the humanism that prevailed in education at that time. By age nineteen, he went to Orleans and Bourges to study law. In 1532, Calvin returned to Paris attending lectures as he pleased in the manner of a "professional student." He had a conversion experience, about which little is known, and "forsook following humanism," and then he left the Catholic Church.[29]

Calvin moved to Basel in Switzerland in 1534 and wrote *The Institutes of the Christian Religion,* which he published at age twenty-six. Unlike most Protestant writings of the day, this was a compendium of Calvin's concept of "true Christianity" rather than a polemic against Rome. His theology was built around his doctrine of God and his attributes.[30] Like Luther, he was influenced by his study of St Augustine concerning human sinfulness. Under the philosophical assumption that nothing can happen without God willing it, he, like Luther, espoused "double predestination,"[31] which claimed that prior to creation God chose which individuals to save and which ones to damn. Calvin taught that at the "fall," in the garden of Eden, man became totally depraved, and this depravity was inherited by all his posterity.

Like Luther and Zwingli, Calvin claimed Sola Scriptura as the only source and standard for Christian doctrine. Likewise he limited the sacraments to the two "dominical" ones commanded by the Lord. He retained infant baptism as bringing one into membership in the Christian Church, but he denied its efficacy to remove the guilt of original sin.[32] He taught that receiving communion confirmed a person's faith but that Jesus was not corporeally present in the bread and wine that had been blessed, but was rather spiritually discerned. Communion was limited to be celebrated four times a year.[33] It has been suggested this was to preclude a loss of reverence due to excessive familiarity from more frequent participation.

In Calvin's reformed church, the other Sundays of the year had a simple specified order of service. This consisted of "invocation, prayer, Confession, absolution to all who were truly repentant, singing the Table of the Law, reading from the Bible, sermon, psalm or hymn, and benediction."[34] Church architecture was affected, in that the central altar was replaced by the pulpit because of the prominent emphasis on the written Word.

Calvin had come to Geneva for a visit, and the resident Reformer, Farel, convinced him to stay, which he did for the next twenty-eight years. There he influenced the local government and eventually crated a "theocratic commonwealth" based on his interpretation of Scripture.[35] In this system, the government had responsibility for most aspects of life and executed punishments, including the death penalty. The Presbyterian Church, as well as many other Protestant denominations, owe their existence to this prodigious Reformer.

The Presbyterians

In Scotland, John Knox was ordained a Catholic priest in 1540, but he later became the prominent leader of Protestant reform after coming under the influence of George Wishart. Wishart, a Scot who had a strong Swiss humanist and Calvinist educational background, came from Switzerland to preach reform in Scotland. Knox, taken up with his ideas, was undeterred when

Wishart was condemned as a heretic and burned at the stake in 1546.[36] In sympathy, Knox began to preach Protestantism, and as a result was arrested and sentenced to nineteen months as a French galley slave.[37] His sentence finished, he fled to Geneva for his safety after the ascension of the Catholic Queen Mary to the English throne.

Having associated personally with Calvin, Knox returned to Scotland in 1555 as a strong Calvinist leader of reform. In 1561 parliament made Scotland officially Protestant and adopted a confession of faith drawn up by Knox and his colleagues. Like Luther, Zwingli, and Calvin, Knox depended on the civil government to enforce his religious policies.[38] He also placed a heavy emphasis on education, which doubtless affected the course of Scotland on the world for the next few centuries.

Nearly a century and a half later, the Scottish government was still under strong religious control by the Kirk (church). It still dealt severely with "heresy" and "blasphemy," as was seen in the case of Thomas Aikenhead. This eighteen-year-old theology student at Edinburgh expressed doubts to his fellow students about the authority of the Bible, miracles, and the reliability of the apostles. He questioned Jesus' resurrection and redemption itself. His "friends" reported him to the Kirk. The Lord Advocate then charged him with blasphemy, which still at that time required the death penalty. Though he repented and recanted, Thomas was still hanged on January 8, 1697 as the required penalty for his crime.[39]

Uniqueness of "Reform" in England

Unlike the Reformation in all the other countries, England had a unique course of separation from Rome. Henry VIII

(1491–1547) became king of England in 1509[40] and married his deceased brother's wife, Catherine of Aragon of the Spanish royal family. Henry was desperate for a male heir to continue his lineage on the throne, but none was forthcoming. In the absence of today's knowledge of genetics, he did not know that he was responsible to provide the "Y" chromosome, and he sought to rid himself of the wife who could not produce a son. A papal annulment was rendered impossible by the political situation between the Holy Roman Emperor, the Vatican, Spain, and England. Henry, though staunchly Catholic, broke relations with Rome and secured an in-house annulment with a now separate, schismatic Catholic Church in England.

He remarried and later produced a son, Edward. The royal succession passed to Edward, the only male heir, who had been raised a Protestant. After young Edward's death, the throne passed to Henry's oldest daughter, Mary, the only surviving child of Catherine of Aragon—and she was Catholic. She was succeeded by her younger sister Elizabeth, daughter of Anne Boleyn. Elizabeth was both practical and reform-minded, therefore under her reign, the end result was a somewhat "Calvinized" Catholic, slightly Protestant Church of England. It retained the apostolic succession; the ministry of bishops, priests, and deacons; and most all the old rituals. The altar remained central in the churches, with the pulpit and reading lectern off to the side. Probably because of the still very Catholic nature of the Church of England, Rome took a couple of centuries before finally pronouncing Anglican Holy Orders to be invalid—they weren't invalidated until 1896.[41] Interestingly, in 2009 Pope Benedict XVI invited Anglicans disaffected by extreme liberalism, to come over under the umbrella of Rome.

What Happened?

As we have looked at the three major Reformers in the progression that led them out of the Catholic Church, it is obvious that each split involved changes in doctrine that sealed the separation. There were also doctrinal incompatibilities among the Reformers themselves. Yet each claimed Scripture as their only source of authority. The significant differences of doctrine from supposedly the same source of authority indicated that a serious problem concerning authority still remained.

In the past, the three-part structure of authority in the Ancient Church had been a source of its strength and stability. The complexity of this triad, with all three strands of episcopacy (the bishops), tradition, and the written Word being in agreement, helped avoid the Church's following "every wind of doctrine" and thereby protected the unity of the body. When there was "sin in the house" over the centuries, it was dealt with, sometimes more effectively than at other times.

The Protestant Reformers viewed the corruption among prelates in the sixteenth-century Renaissance Church as justification to reject the triad of authority and replace it. In doing so, they abandoned the direct historic continuity of the Church to the apostles. This was replaced by "the minister" whose authorization was of variable etiology.

The tradition of the apostles, which included details of the gospel message, also included information beyond what was written down in Scripture, such as the details of "how to minister" and "how to choose and authorize" new ministers and perform sacraments. Protestant Reformers considered this to be simply "tradition of man."

The changes they made were major. Total authority was now deemed to reside in the Bible *alone*. This essentially made the new denominations "people of the book." Five ancient sacraments were rejected as such, which involved doctrinal changes, but by whose authority? The altar was eliminated and the pulpit placed front and center, reflecting the intellectualization of the faith as the focus was put on preaching. The result was a significantly different church from that of the previous fifteen hundred years. The question that begs to be answered, in the light of the huge increase of divisions during the last five hundred years, is: were all—or some—or any—of these changes truly justified?

CHAPTER 9

THE RADICAL REFORMATION

The Radical Reformation comprised the third phase of Church reforms in the sixteenth century. Its leaders undertook even more extreme changes because they considered the efforts of the major Reformers to be inadequate in the quest for an unblemished New Testament faith and worship. A large number of individual thinkers and leaders were of this persuasion. The movement is of particular importance because it is the source of almost all evangelical Christian denominations today.

As a general class, the Radical Reformers were called "Anabaptists" because of their insistence on re-baptizing converts from other churches who were baptized as infants. They believed that, because infants were not capable of understanding the faith as required for a "believer's baptism," they were to be excluded from this rite.

The Radical Reform movement is considered to have begun in Switzerland under Conrad Grebel (1498–1526), who had been a student at Basel, Vienna, and Paris under liberal humanist professors. He moved to Zurich and came under the influence of Zwingli, and then had a conversion experience. The two became friends but drifted apart because Grebel was impatient with Zwingli for moving too conservatively.[1] Grebel and his friend Felix Manz gathered a like-minded group called "the Swiss Brethren," whose aim was to return to the simplicity of the Church of apostolic times in its organization and worship.[2] By 1534, Grebel and Manz came to the conclusion that infant baptism was unscriptural. In January 1525, the Zurich city council rejected their ideas. In spite of this, the two men had themselves re-baptized, along with others, an event which marks the official beginning of the Anabaptist movement.[3]

The Zurich council and the Reformed Church in Zurich, where Zwingli was the reform leader, were strong supporters of infant baptism and consequently became enemies of the Anabaptist movement. Zwingli and his supporters prevailed on the city council to order the Swiss Brethren to disband. In 1525, the council decreed that all un-baptized children must be baptized or suffer banishment.[4]

Unwelcome in Zurich, Grebel, and Manz and their associates moved on to other cities in Switzerland. By now they had also come to reject predestination and the doctrine of the total depravity of man and had accepted the doctrine of "free will" instead. These ideas defied Protestant doctrine as taught by Luther, Calvin, Zwingli, and others. Grebel and Manz and associates were later imprisoned in Zurich because of teaching "believer's baptism," although Grebel and Manz managed to escape.

In 1526, the Zwinglian mainline Protestants, as represented by the Zurich city fathers, were so opposed to "believer's baptism" that they criminalized Anabaptist doctrine. It was considered "sedition," or rebellion, which was sufficiently serious for the government to require the death penalty by decapitation, burning, or now by drowning.[5] This last method was possibly inspired by the Anabaptist practice of baptism by total immersion. In 1527, Manz was recaptured and executed by drowning. It is noteworthy that Luther and Melanchthon in Germany at first opposed the death penalty for Anabaptists but later came to agree to it because of the seriousness of sedition.[6] This was in effect a Protestant Inquisition which showed no more mercy than the Catholic Inquisition in "stamping out error."

There was an extreme range of beliefs and doctrines among different leaders of the Anabaptist movement, which grew strong in Germany, Holland, Moravia, and Austria. Some of the leaders even rejected the Trinity, and others rejected the divinity of Jesus. In Germany, Thomas Munzer was convinced he was called to set up a "new apostolic kingdom."[7] His disciple, Hans Hut in Moravia, was even more extreme. He taught that the kingdom could be hastened by extermination of the wicked, a sort of sixteenth-century Christian jihad.[8]

Another leader, also in Moravia, was of a different persuasion. Jacob Wiedemann taught pacifism and a return to communal ownership of all possessions, just as seen in the book of Acts.[9] His movement was in sharp contrast to that of Hut and Munzer. Many other sectarian movements between these extremes were the forerunners of many of today's denominations.

More Anabaptist Splintering

Another Anabaptist leader was Menno Simmons[10] (1496–1561). He was ordained a Catholic priest in 1524 and within a year began to doubt the validity of the Mass and then to question infant baptism. He remained in the Catholic Church until 1536 when he was re-baptized and became an Anabaptist minister. He married and had a family, though he faced the threat of persecution from both Rome and the Lutherans. He became a notable leader of the movement in the Netherlands and Germany and acquired a large following. Upon his death, his followers were called Mennonites.[11] There was no definite unity of doctrine among the Mennonites, and multiple confessions of faith were in use. To the present, they persist in significant numbers.

Jacob Ammann led another branch of Mennonites near the close of the seventeenth century which focused on a more strict discipline. These have persisted to the present as the Amish. Large numbers of them live in Pennsylvania, Indiana, and Ohio at present.[12] Even today, for fear of the temptation to idolatry of graven images, their children's dolls have no faces, and they possess no mirrors or pictures to preclude the risk of idolization.

During the Reformation, Jacob Hutter led another branch of Anabaptists who lived in community, seeking to replicate the first church in the book of Acts. Living together, they owned everything in common. Jacob was hunted down under order of the emperor, Ferdinand of Austria. He was caught, tortured, and burned to death in 1536, for being an Anabaptist leader.[13] After his death, his followers were called Hutterites, and because of persecution by both Protestants and Catholics, they spread out a great distance in seeking refuge. Today Hutterite colonies are found in many places in North and South America.[14]

Rise of the Baptists

Today, Baptists are the largest modern Protestant denomination in America. They also trace back to the sixteenth century. In England, unlike the Puritans who aimed to reform the Church of England into a "proper Protestant church," the Anabaptists chose instead to exit the established church and to keep authority vested in the local congregation.[15] When the Catholic Queen Mary ascended the throne, many Protestants fled to the Netherlands. In 1609, it was among these that John Smyth formed the first Baptist congregation. His associate,

Thomas Helwys, returned to England and established a Baptist congregation near London in 1612. Despite facing prejudice there, they grew to seven congregations by 1630 in the London area.[16]

Baptists accepted much of Reformed theology, including the Trinity and the authority of the Bible alone as well as priesthood of all believers. They did differ amongst themselves concerning predestination and free will. They fell into two groups, "the Particular" and "the General," terms identifying whom Jesus died for. The Particular Baptists thought he died only for the elect. The General Baptists believed he died for all men.[17]

The early Baptists also rejected sacraments in the traditional sense, accepting baptism and the Lord's Supper as "ordinances" since they were "ordered" or commanded by Jesus. For the Lord's Supper, they held the Zwinglian view of a memorial meal in remembrance of the meal Jesus shared with the apostles the night he was betrayed.[18] There was no sense of Real Presence, spiritual or otherwise. Baptism was understood as a public affirmation by the individual of the faith he possessed. It was believer's baptism and not administered to infants, and it conferred no special grace. The mode was by total immersion in keeping with Paul's description of being buried with Christ and rising to new life.[19] Some Baptists considered a third ordinance of "foot washing."

The Baptist movement spread to America, in Rhode Island in 1639, and has grown steadily since then.[20] Baptists emphasize the autonomy of the local congregation, and many have their own "statement of faith" which might differ slightly from that of a different congregation. A very large percentage of evangelicals are Baptist. It is the largest Protestant denomination in America, with a membership reported to be in the order of 30–40 million.[21]

Pentecostals

Outside of the Mainline Protestant churches, hundreds of denominations exist, tracing their roots back to various groups in the Reformation. One of these, Pentecostals, make up a significant portion of the highly visible Protestant evangelical churches in America. *Nelson's Guide to Denominations* traces Pentecostalism to the beginning of the last century, having its roots in the Holiness Movement that resulted from John Wesley's teaching on sanctification. In December 1900, Charles Parham, an ex-Methodist teacher in a Kansas Holiness Bible School, had his students research the New Testament concerning the "Baptism of the Holy Spirit." They discovered that in every instance, it was accompanied by speaking in tongues. On New Year's Eve 1900, Parham and his students gathered to pray for this experience for themselves.[22] Their prayer was answered.

Parham subsequently went on a preaching tour to the neighboring states, sharing this experience and then founding a new Bible school in Houston, Texas. He defied social tradition by accepting an African-American Methodist preacher, William Seymour, as a student. Before speaking in tongues himself, Seymour accepted a pastorate in a church in California but was soon dismissed for preaching about speaking in tongues. He then founded a mission on Azusa Street in Los Angeles, from which the Pentecostal experience spread worldwide.[23]

Perhaps because of the manifestations of the Holy Spirit such as "being slain in the Spirit" and speaking in tongues, as well as their more exuberant worship styles, mainline churches at first disdained Pentecostals as "Holy Rollers." Those individuals who were members of Episcopal, Methodist, or other mainline churches who became involved in this new movement were frequently expelled from their congregations or else voluntarily departed under duress and formed new Pentecostal denominations.[24] Such denominations as the Assemblies of God and the Foursquare Church became prominent among these. As these Pentecostal denominations matured, the radical manifestations of the Spirit declined, so that when the Charismatic Renewal came alive in the 1960s, there was some jealousy expressed over Catholics now speaking in tongues and prophesying more than old-school Pentecostals were!

The Charismatic Churches: A Midcentury Movement

Generally speaking, the theology of Protestant churches tends to reject the "sign gifts" of the Holy Spirit such as those listed in 1 Corinthians 12:8–10: word of wisdom, word of knowledge, gift of faith, gift of healing, miracles, prophecy, gift of tongues, and interpretation of tongues. The mainline leaders felt that these gifts had ceased with the death of the apostles. This view is often justified by quoting 1 Corinthians 13:8–10 to indicate that prophecy, tongues, and knowledge would cease once perfection comes. Some insist that the advent of the New Testament fulfilled this and eliminated the further need for these gifts.

Once again, there is more behind this belief than just a simple interpretation of the Bible. Most of the reform-minded through the years have been hesitant to acknowledge any validity to the performance of miracles by Catholic saints over the centuries. Remember that the Catholic Church has a sacrament (Confirmation) for the infilling of the Holy Spirit, imparted by the laying on of hands. It is like Paul did at Ephesus: "The moment Paul laid hands on them the Holy Spirit came down on them, and they began to speak in tongues and prophesy" (Acts 19:6). For many Protestants, admitting the presence of supernatural activity from God among Catholics would be tantamount to accepting the validity of the Roman Catholic Church.

From the 1960s through the 1980s, there was a widespread movement of charismatic renewal among some within the Protestant mainline churches as well as the Roman Catholic Church. At the time, there was unprecedented cross-denominational cooperation and building of relationships. Speakers from multiple denominations addressed Charismatic conferences. The Full Gospel Businessmen Fellowship International was open to all denominations, and some local chapter boards had both Catholic and Protestant members on the same board. But the momentum of the Charismatic movement in North America seemed to flag as the 1980s progressed, and the interdenominational cooperation has faded considerably.

Nelson's Guide notes that many who experienced renewal stayed in their original denominations, but many others, for various reasons, departed and formed new Charismatic denominations. Some ministries became independent megachurches. Others formed over a hundred new denominations.[25]

Independent Churches

Nondenominational and Independent churches came into existence long before the Charismatic Renewal movement. This was primarily a reaction to the Modernism that swept through many of the mainline churches in the nineteenth and twentieth centuries. The advent of Darwinism in the mid-nineteenth century had followed on from the intellectual period of the Enlightenment, which advanced the cause of secular humanism that continued on from the Renaissance. No area of intellectual endeavor was immune from being called into question. As a result, the Modernist controversy of the early twentieth-century was empowered.

In Modernism's early days, traditional theological assumptions were rocked by scientific biblical criticism and the demythologizing of the Gospels by critics from the inside, along with Darwinism, psychology, and sociology from the outside.[26] The resulting controversy among theologians was whether to capitulate to the critics or depart from the mainline denominations that espoused Modernism. Those who left their denominations formed many small or independent churches and ministries. Many of these neo-evangelicals were served by Fuller Seminary in California for the training of ministers.[27] The Vineyard Church denomination, associated with John Wimber, has become quite prominent among these.

Radical Changes

Just as the mainline Protestant Reformers made major changes to doctrine and organization in their departure from the Catholic Church, the Radical Reformation made significant changes as they moved even further beyond the mainline denominations. Where the mainline Reformers reduced the number of sacraments, very early on, most of the Anabaptists movement rejected sacraments completely and replaced them with ordinances, being understood as commands of Scripture. Almost without exception, they also adopted believer's baptism, based on the New Testament examples of people first hearing the gospel and then responding by being baptized. They also insisted on total immersion, which is implied but not specifically commanded in the Bible.

The humanist revolution of the Renaissance emphasized the competence of the human intellect along with a spirit of independence and individualism. Church reformation was markedly influenced by this cultural trend, which inspired the freedom to challenge and question the authority of Church leaders and the validity of ancient doctrines. This influenced the major Reformers in their assessment of the Catholic Church and likewise the Radical Reformers as they reassessed the coexisting mainline Reformation. It provided the inspiration for increased decentralization of Church authority and independence of the local congregation.

All of the Protestant Reformers, the major ones as well as the radical ones, were in good faith seeking to return to the purity of the New Testament church. The accepted theory was that the Bible, being God's Word, was an adequate source of authority and the only source of true doctrine and practice. The right of the individual to interpret it was a jealously guarded principle of the Protestant and Radical Reformations, which followed from the principle of the priesthood of all believers. However, instead of producing unity among believers, a multiplication of differing interpretations and doctrine arose. The result was a splintering frenzy of new independent denominations.

At the end of the first fifteen hundred years of the existence of the Church, there were only two churches, with almost identical doctrine. From the sixteenth century to the present, there was an exponential growth of new denominations, now numbering in the tens of thousands. These, for the most part, are independent of each other. The scandal of enmity has infected many of the relationships among them. Even today, open prejudice and hostility persists among some denominations, who claim many of the other ones are not even truly Christian. Yet every Protestant denomination believes in, or at least gives lip service to, using the Bible as their only source of authority.

If we truly accept the Bible as God's inerrant Word, being divinely inspired, we are obliged to consider it as a true source of authority. The problem arises from the lack of a unified interpretation. No two people will have the identical educational experience even at the same university! The variety of professors gives students a veritable menu of ways of thinking. Each student therefore develops a unique outlook, even if it is similar to others in his class. That is how Zwingli and Luther had such different opinions. The universal adoption of Sola Scriptura by the Protestant Reformation in the sixteenth century marks the turning point, the beginning of a cascade into multiple denominations. It is not *Scriptura* that was the cause of these divisions. It is obvious that the culprit was the acceptance of *Sola* as an "immutable dogma" without a universal standard of interpretation. Instead, doctrines remain at the mercy of variable educational traditions.

Today, it would appear as if the powers of hell have driven wedges between each of the special callings and giftings in the Church, cutting it into tiny pieces so the parts can no longer function as a body. Each denomination or congregation may have a valuable divinely offered gift or special calling, but it is devoid of the strengths of the other gifts distributed among the thousands of disconnected denominations.

Such a dismembered body is not what Jesus prayed for. In a day when conservative Christians are culturally disdained and maligned by the media, and laws are passed requiring us to act contrary to our religious faith, the whole body of Christ needs to speak out. How can a sack of body parts do this—or anything else?

CHAPTER 10

SOLA SCRIPTURA

Of all the changes made by the Protestant Reformation, the adoption of Scripture as the sole source of authority was the keystone. It was eagerly embraced by every Reformer of every variety. This concept was used to justify all the other changes made in the Protestant departure from the Catholic Church.

The view of the Bible as sole source did not originate with the Protestant Reformers of the sixteenth century. We have already met Peter Waldo, a Catholic layman in France who in 1170 gathered a band of lay preachers and denied needing the authority of the Church, defending himself by claiming to need to obey only the authority of Scripture.[1] Another pre-Reformation voice for Sola Scriptura was John Wycliffe (1320–1384), a Catholic priest and Oxford professor in England[2] who was associated closely with the government in its political controversy with the papacy. He was likely influenced by the intellectual tenor of the twelfth-century Renaissance in the development of his new theological ideas. He came to consider the visible Church to be a human invention and its "true membership" to be known to God alone. He eventually believed Church organization and ritual were "traditional accretions,"[3] and he defended his new ideas by claiming Scripture as his sole authority.[4] Both Wycliffe and Waldo challenged the authority of the Catholic Church and are considered heroes of the faith by Protestants because of their stand concerning the Bible as sole authority.

Yet, the Catholic Church also believes the Bible to be divinely inspired and an inerrant and reliable source of truth. In the Catechism we read:

> God is the author of Sacred Scripture . . . Holy Mother Church, relying on the faith of the apostolic age, accepts as sacred and canonical the books of the Old and the New Testaments, whole and entire, with all their parts, on the grounds that, written under the inspiration of the Holy Spirit, have God as their author and have been handed on as such to the Church herself.[5]

By this we can see that the Catholic Church is as much a "Bible-believing church" as any evangelical church. In the light of this fact, there has to be some explanation for the different paths of doctrine taken by each side. The Bible, especially the New Testament, is agreed upon, but the problem is to discern whether "sola" is adequate for the total source of doctrine. Therefore, we must look further in order to assess the evidence. If "sola" is inadequate, we need to search for what is missing.

The Intention of Holy Scripture

Part of the difference between the paths taken may originate from a different understanding of the intention of Scripture. Examining the contents of the Bible, we can see that it consists of stories of God interacting with heroes of the faith, of history, poetry, prophecy, and all the good and bad that happened to the people of God.

Over many centuries, Moses, the prophets, and others wrote down their encounters with God. History and poetry (or psalms) were part of this collection revered by Israel. The early versions were written in Hebrew or Aramaic and later translated into Greek as the Septuagint, so named from the rounding out of the number of scholars who did the translation, LXX being the Roman numerals for this number. This Greek version was the original Old Testament of the Church, and as such, it was the source of Old Testament quotations made by the writers of the New Testament.

It does not pretend to be a science book, nor a "how-to" manual (aside from Leviticus and other books or passages detailing priestly duties and rituals in ancient Israel). Although it offers many instructions on how to live a godly life, the Bible is more of a record of the interaction between God and humanity. All the sordid details of human frailty and rebellion are given in a graphic manner. The heart of God and his character are seen in his forgiveness and the lengths to which he went to rescue those whom he created in his own image. Ultimately, it is a love story of cosmic proportions.

It is important to note what the Bible has to say about itself. The Scripture the apostles knew and used was the LXX. Hardly any of the New Testament had been written when Paul was evangelizing and writing letters. It would be another 350 years before the content of the New Testament would be culled out from the many Christian (and quasi-Christian) writings extant at the time and then assembled and approved as Scripture. The apostolic writings were in use in the Church long before that official stamp of approval and the closure of the canon, yet, after saying all this, we are unable to find any place where the Bible claims to be the only source of authority for the Church.

The Bible does, however, state its purpose. In Paul's letter to Timothy we read:

> You must keep to what you have been taught and know to be true; remember who your teachers were, and how, ever since you were a child you have known the holy scriptures [i.e. the LXX]—from these you can learn the wisdom that leads to salvation through faith in Christ Jesus. All scripture is inspired by God and can be profitably used for teaching, for refuting error, for guiding people's lives and teaching them to be holy. (2 Timothy 3:14–16)

Here we see that Paul did not limit Timothy to using only Scripture in his teaching, but he urged him to pass on to his hearers the *tradition* Paul had taught ("remember who your teachers were"). Timothy was essentially being told to teach the tradition he had learned from Paul and to use Scripture (the LXX) as well, to help with teaching, correcting, and guiding.

Paul also wrote to Titus about the importance of tradition in stating the qualifications for ordaining an elder: "He must have a firm grasp of the unchanging message of the tradition" (Titus 1:9). The "message of the tradition" was the gospel story, as well as the details of how to lead the local church where the elder was going to be placed in charge. The elder would have to have information well beyond the written words of the LXX, which could convey nothing of Jesus' life or teachings. At that point in time there was as yet no New Testament because much of it still needed to be written, probably including the four gospels.

For the next fifteen hundred years (and to our time too) the LXX provided the source of the forty-six books of the Old

Testament. The Protestant Reformers rejected seven of these books, as well as portions of Esther and Daniel, which they judged were not sufficiently inspired. Yet at the same time, after reducing the Old Testament content, they still insisted Scripture was their sole authority.

The New Testament and Individual Interpretation

The right of the individual to interpret the Bible has been accepted by every Protestant movement since the Reformation. We ought to ask what the Bible has to say about how it is to be interpreted. In Acts 8:27–38, we find the story of Philip meeting the treasurer of the queen of Ethiopia along the road. This man was reading from Isaiah, and Philip asked him if he understood what he was reading. He replied, "How can I unless I have someone to guide me?" Philip explained the passage and the man, having now understood, desired to be baptized.

The apostle Peter also talks about interpretation in his second letter. He commends the use of scriptural prophecy as a lamp but warns, "At the same time, we must be most careful to remember that the interpretation of scriptural prophecy is never a matter for the individual" (2 Peter 1:20). This verse does not lend much support for the "right of individual interpretation." Human nature tends to make us selective readers of Scripture. We emphasize the verses that support our own theological understanding and at the same time tend to minimize or overlook those that disagree with our position.

In both of these examples from the New Testament, it is obvious that the Bible itself indicates that assistance from outside the written text can be of significant help to fully understand what is intended to be communicated. Without Philip, the Ethiopian treasurer would have remained confused. The admonition of Peter about private interpretation serves to deter speculation, which speaks directly to our own day with its controversy over such things as end-times prophecy "timelines."

Inevitability of Interpretation

Language is always subject to interpretation. The different nuances of words and cultures can convey more than one way to understand what is being communicated, even when you are speaking the same language. In England, to say a girl is "homely" would be a sort of compliment, but in America it would be an insult. When it comes to discussing spirituality, educational background determines much of what you understand by the meaning of words and concepts. For instance, when Scripture says "election," a person schooled in a philosophy that emphasizes the idea of the divine attribute of immutability will understand the word to mean that predestination has an inevitable outcome. One schooled in thinking that endorses free will would interpret election as having a generalized meaning, allowing for a possible change of outcome. Both our educational background and our religious presuppositions will influence what we understand by what we read.

The act of translating from one language to another provides an even greater opportunity for interpretive differences, since translators can utilize words that slant the meaning of the original text into something different in the new language. For example, the quotation from 2 Timothy we noted above translates the word *didaskalian* as "teaching" in both the Jerusalem Bible and the NASB. The KJV and the the NKJV both translate that word as "doctrine." The Greek Lexicon[6] gives the possible English meanings in descending order as *the act of teaching, information, instruction, matter of thought,* and lists *doctrine* as the last. The root Greek word from which it is derived is *didasko,* which means "to teach." This may seem like a small point, but it does have implications as to interpretation. It is the difference between Paul advising Timothy to use God-inspired Scripture as valuable for his teaching activity versus inferring that Scripture is to be the only source for doctrine and practice of the faith. At that point in history, "Scripture" was just the Old Testament.

In *World Magazine*, Emily Belz reported a less subtle example of doctrinal changes via translation in a Turkish-language version of the gospel of Matthew in 2011. Frontiers Translators, in conjunction with SIL, a translation partner with Wycliffe Bible Translators, produced a "conservative, Muslim-friendly" version that referred to God the Father as "the Great Protector" and Jesus as "God's Representative."[7] Obviously this attempt to make the gospel more acceptable to Muslims expresses radical changes to the meaning, and therefore the impact, of the gospel.

Something Missing?

It may seem sacrilegious to say that something is missing in Scripture, but the Bible itself says so. The gospel of John, in concluding, states that the apostles had many more experiences with Jesus, but they were not included in what was written down. The things that *were* written were put there for the purpose of helping the reader "believe that Jesus is the Son of God and that he can have life through his name" (John 20:30–31). From this, we could conclude that the other authors of the New Testament also experienced much more than they committed to pen and paper. The rest of the story they undoubtedly communicated orally, and this would have included much of the "tradition" that Paul referred to in his letters.

It is significant that the explosion in the number of denominations began in the sixteenth century when the Protestant

Reformation had newly espoused Sola Scriptura. By limiting their source of authority to the written Bible text alone, they rejected the authority of episcopacy and the apostolic tradition, which along with Scripture had previously comprised the authority structure that successfully discouraged division within the Church. Prior to the Reformation, all the details concerning things alluded to but never fully explained in Scripture were provided by the apostolic tradition as the "teaching of the Church." By omitting the tradition, the relevance of these allusions risks being lost.

When Martin Luther coined the phrases "Sola Fide" and "Sola Scriptura," I'm sure he was trying to express the extreme, critical importance of faith and of Scripture. Unfortunately, the word "sola" or "alone" in the last analysis is insufficient, since every concept we learn comes through the lens, or filter, of what our teachers taught us. If, for instance, we reject the lens of tradition and episcopacy, a vacuum is left that demands to be filled in order to make sense of what is alluded to in Scripture. Different nuances of education lead to different interpretations, which risk being in disagreement with one another. What standard of interpretation should we agree to use, and how should we determine it?

We shall consider four scriptural allusions that are directly involved with the Protestant Reformation. These are 1) the nature of God, 2) the acquisition of salvation, 3) the nature of the ministry in the New Testament or Early Church, and 4) the order of worship. Each of these is alluded to in the New Testament with scanty details given in the text.

Allusion 1: The Doctrine of the Trinity

The Father, the Son, and the Holy Spirit are mentioned quite frequently in our New Testament. Scripture seems to take for granted that the reader will understand. The idea of "one God in three Persons" is not specifically spelled out, nor does the word "Trinity" occur in the Bible. Yet this doctrine is accepted by almost all who claim the name of Christian. The major Reformers and most of the Radical Reformers accepted this doctrine in approximately the same way as the Orthodox and the Catholic Churches. Yet, to articulate belief in the Trinity as "one God in three Persons" does require understanding beyond the written text of the Bible. Those who believe this doctrine are actually utilizing the authority of Church tradition, whether they realize it or not—even though tradition was supposedly rejected by the Reformation.

Allusion 2: Salvation and Predestination

The New Testament is very clear that salvation is by grace and faith as a result of the cross. However, some of the leaders of the Reformation went well beyond the allusion in Scripture concerning election when they described salvation. The Old Testament "election" references pertain specifically to the Messiah or to the people of Israel as a nation. The New Testament has twenty-six references to "elect" or "chosen," but there is no detail given to explain what these words mean. Wycliffe, Luther, and Calvin all originally seriously held to the doctrine of "double predestination," first implied by St Augustine of Hippo but never adopted by the Church as doctrine.[8] The concept is that prior to creation, God decided on exactly which individuals would be saved and which would be condemned to hell. The choice was irrevocable.

However, a typical use of the word "chosen" in the New Testament occurs in the letter of 2 John, which refers to both the sending and receiving congregations as being "chosen." In Colossians, the recipients of the letter are referred to as "God's chosen race" (Colossians 3:12). The Greek word used is *eklektoi,* which the lexicon renders as "picked, select, specially beloved, precious."[9] All the twenty-six New Testament references always refer to a people or a group. There is no mention of choosing individuals for damnation. The concept of double predestination requires going beyond Sola Scriptura by utilizing philosophy with which both St. Augustine and the men of the Renaissance took for granted as part of their worldview.

The irrevocable nature of predestination depends on the Greek philosophical understanding that God is "immutable." That means he can't be changed; a philosophical attribute of "true deity." Therefore, because God is also omnipotent, nothing can happen without God willing it, so whatever happens, he has willed it. (This Greek philosophical concept is more properly called fatalism.)

There is presently a tendency to treat prophecy in the same fatalistic manner, especially in the book of Revelation, viewing end-time prophecies as "fate on rails." It is too easy to miss the *IF* in prophecy. In Revelation 2:5, the Ephesians are told that *if* they do not repent they will lose their lamp-stand. In Jeremiah 18 at the potter's shed, God tells Jeremiah that when he plans destruction for a nation, *if* they repent and change, God says "I then change my mind." Remember that the God of the Bible does not fit easily into the categories of Greek, or any other philosophy! After all, Christianity is a Jewish religion.

Allusion 3: The Nature of Ministry

In the New Testament there are multiple references not only to apostles but also to bishops (*episkopos*), elders (*presbuteros*), and deacons (*diakanos*), especially in the epistles. There is little information as to the exact role of each of these ministers. First

Timothy and Titus include a list of the qualifications, but without detail as to the method of choosing or of ordaining elders, to say nothing of what such people are expected to do in that role. In the first chapter of Acts, the selection of Matthias to replace Judas as an apostle was done by casting lots. This is reminiscent of the Urim and Thumim[10] in the Old Testament, used for determining the will of God. The actual details concerning these areas of ministry, regarding the specific nature of the duties, authority, and responsibilities for each one, are dealt with only in the writings of the successors to the apostles.

Perhaps it is because these offices of ministry are lacking so much specific detail in the Bible that all the Protestant Reformers discarded them. Most of the modern denominations today have a "minister" or "pastor," but how does that individual connect with the authority given to the apostles and in turn passed on down? Many denominations have noticed the titles of elder and deacon in Scripture and so have created a "board of elders" or a "board of deacons" to assist the pastor. Some modern Baptists and Pentecostals now have bishops who wear purple clerical garb but avoid claiming apostolic succession as the Catholics, Orthodox, and Anglicans do.

Allusion 4: The Plan and Order of Worship

Only in the Old Testament is much significant information given concerning forms of worship. For instance, in Leviticus 16:11–23 we find details about the offering of incense and the utilization of a bull and goats in the ritual of atonement for the priest and also for the people. The New Testament makes reference to Early Church worship, but with very scanty detail. In Acts 20, there is mention of their meeting the first day of the week to "break bread." In Acts 2:42 we read that "they continued in the apostles doctrine, fellowship, the breaking of bread and the prayers" (KJV). Most commentators recognize the breaking of bread as referring to the Lord's Supper. The Bible gives no detail as to just how it was carried out.

Many modern evangelicals and pastors, like their predecessors, express a desire to return to the New Testament pattern of worship. They picture a return to the simplicity of the Early Church under the assumption that additions and corruptions have occurred over the centuries due to the Catholic Church.

Yet, when researching into history we always try to locate the earliest source, closest to the event which we are studying, in order to acquire the most reliable information about it. Earlier we noted that in 155 AD Justin Martyr wrote in detail about the ritual of the Eucharist.[11] It included the reading of Scriptures, preaching, prayer over bread and wine, and distribution of communion. He specifically noted that the blessed bread and wine were not considered common bread and wine, but the body and blood of the Lord.[12]

Such normal Sunday worship at this very early period seems complex and unfamiliar to many younger evangelicals, but for the Catholic, Orthodox, or Anglican, this liturgy is still the normal experience every Sunday. Obviously then, Catholic worship has not evolved from simple to complex during the first sixteen centuries, but instead it is Protestant worship which has generally become less liturgical and less complex over the last five hundred years. Indeed, it would appear that there has been a devolution rather than an evolution during this latest time period. Undoubtedly, our presumption of "increasing complexity" in Church practice is driven by an underlying faith in Enlightenment philosophy, and we take it for granted because it is a subliminal part of our culture.

"Sola" Impossible?

When something is mentioned in Scripture without much detail, we should suspect there could be a reason that detail is omitted. The most probable reason is that of familiarity. It is certain that the Early Church congregations were totally familiar with the detail of the orders of ministry, the liturgy ritual, and most of basic Christian doctrine, so the writers of the New Testament had no need to record what everyone took for granted. The allusion itself was a sufficient reminder of what they already knew. However, when the culture changes, we risk losing some of these assumed details. The teaching of the Church tradition had kept them alive in the Catholic and Orthodox Churches. The relative rapidity of cultural change wrought by the Renaissance offered alternatives to the "old tradition" and encouragement to question it.

The scriptural allusions we have so far considered illustrate the fact that the Protestant Reformers were obliged to go beyond Sola Scriptura to arrive at the conclusions they made. The acceptance of the doctrine of the Trinity in a sense appropriated Catholic Church tradition for details not found in the Bible. In a similar manner, the typical Protestant "double predestination" usage of the scriptural allusion to election involved utilizing concepts of deity derived from Greek philosophy. The development of this doctrine somehow overlooked such New Testament texts as when Jesus said, "It is never the will of your Father in heaven that one of these little ones should be lost" (Matthew 18:14). Paul told Timothy that God "wants everyone to be saved and reach full knowledge of the truth" (Timothy 2:4). Peter wrote, "The Lord is not being slow to carry out his promises . . . wanting nobody to be lost and everybody to be brought to change his ways" (2 Peter 3:9).

The Reformers rejected the threefold ministry of bishop, elder (or priest), and deacon mentioned in the New Testament. However, they replaced them with the new tradition of "the minister," a role more in tune with the academic views of the Renaissance.

If Protestantism didn't get all of its distinctives straight from the Bible, then, it's fair to ask where they *did* get them. It bears pointing out that it was not the worldview of the "interactive" Jewish God of Abraham that prevailed in the sixteenth-century universities. Rather, the well-defined familiar deities of Greek religious philosophy from antiquity, and their associated worldviews, were the ones that popularly prevailed during the Renaissance. It is significant that education is the filter through which our knowledge is acquired and expressed. Almost all Reformers were trained to one degree or another within this Renaissance milieu.

The hope of Sola Scriptura was that the written word by itself would be the standard. In reality, *sola* proved to be illusory.

Instead of producing unity among Protestants, the adoption of Sola Scriptura opened the door to unheard-of degrees of division. The rejection of the apostolic succession in the episcopate and the traditions passed down by the Church left a void which was just begging to be filled. The varieties of educational background within Renaissance universities and worldviews were ready to fill the gap.

Over the intervening centuries, the influence of the Renaissance spirit of independence has prevailed in the education of leaders. Somehow Jesus's prayer for us all to be one in him has been overshadowed by our quest to promote our own "true doctrine" and "biblical worship practice" as we "correctly" interpret it. Could it be true today that the loyalty to the founders of denominations is stronger than our loyalty to the will of Jesus?

CHAPTER 11

SOLA FIDE

For by grace you have been saved through faith; and that not of yourselves, it is the gift of God; not as a result of works, so that no one may boast. (Ephesians 2:8–10, NASB)

The upright man finds life through faith. (Romans 1:17)

"Justification by faith alone" was Martin Luther's expression, and it ultimately fueled the Protestant Reformation. The Church since the time of the apostles had taught a close relationship between faith and living a life acceptable to God. The use of the word "alone" was Luther's innovation. Our concern here is whether or not Luther's insight was an adequate expression for the achievement of justification. Was faith a key ingredient, or was it the *only* ingredient?

Because faith has been so important since the beginning of the Church, the manner in which it is understood is critical. The role of "sola fide" at the beginning of the Protestant Reformation marks the starting point for the cascade of denominational division in Western Christianity. Its definition in the life of faith and in salvation is crucial to fully understand its significance for the Church being "one Body."

What Is Faith?

A Sunday school teacher once asked what faith means, and a little boy replied, "Believing something you know isn't true."[1] Our contemporary culture has considerable ambiguity about the meaning of faith. All children are familiar with the world of make-believe, and even as adults, it colors our idea of the meaning of "believe." Hollywood movies usually portray faith as wishful thinking concerning what everyone knows is impossible.

Theology professor Craig Keener noted how the cultural understanding of faith has infected Christian theology: "Often we also think of faith as a mental state void of doubt that we can work ourselves into."[2] He then goes on to contrast this view with real Christian faith: "yet real faith is a confidence in the loving God we know because we have an intimate relationship with him."

Academia and Faith

Our culture confusion about faith has not come out of a vacuum. Intellectuals, philosophers, and theologians have frequently come to conclusions about faith that resemble our cultural views. Søren Kierkegaard (1813–1855), a philosopher/theologian, thought that Christianity was "composed of opposites which could not be reconciled . . . here at once is an affront to human reason and an object of saving faith."[3] He reconciled this by his famous "leap of faith," that "sacrificed human intellect" by taking a gamble on the "affront to human reason" to grasp the hope of salvation.

Academics often require that faith be unverifiable in order to be defined as faith, since verification would make it a proven fact and not a reasonless trust you can leap into. Atheist Richard

Dawkins, author of *The God Delusion,* presents his own picture of faith in a discussion of the "theory of religion":

> Faith (belief without evidence) is a virtue. The more your beliefs defy the evidence, the more virtuous you are. Virtuoso believers who can manage to believe something really weird, unsupported and insupportable, in the teeth of evidence and reason, are specially highly rewarded.[4]

This is the common cultural, politically correct assessment of faith today for much of academia, science, arts, and media. Might it not be more appropriate for this virtuoso believing to apply to Darwinian evolution and its belief in the exquisite creative power of "chaos (or chance) multiplied by time"?

What you believe does matter. Marcion, in the days of the Early Church, taught that the God of the Old Testament was an inferior deity and that the good God, Jesus, came to man's rescue and was crucified by followers of the God of the Old Testament. Interestingly, Marcion taught that Jesus only required "simple faith" to escape this evil deity.[5] Faith in such a false religious mix won't result in salvation, no matter how strongly one were to believe in it, even if it were an expression of "faith alone."

Facets of Christian Faith

Obviously, believing something that is untrue would be to deceive ourselves. To believe something purely on the basis of a persuasive speaker would make us gullible. Truth does matter. Conversely, the simple believing of facts alone is inadequate to describe Christian faith as it relates to justification. It is imperative to know exactly what we mean by the word "faith" and the mechanism by which it relates to justification.

The dictionary identifies five aspects of faith, in the theological sense, which are applicable to Christian faith:

- Firm belief in what another is saying.
- Theological assent to revelation.
- Intellectual conviction based on evidence.
- Obligation of a relationship of fidelity.
- A doctrinal system.

The apostles were the original messengers who introduced people to the gospel story, and we trust the truthfulness of what they saw and heard. They can only be verified indirectly in that we do not expect them to have been willing to be martyred if they were lying.

In the epistle to the Hebrews we are told, "Faith is the substance of things hoped for and the evidence of things not seen" (Hebrews 11:1, KJV). Also, Jesus said, "Believe it on the evidence of this work, if for no other reason" (John 14:11). Unlike the "faith" of the atheist Richard Dawkins, Christian faith is rooted in historical fact. Scripture strongly supports such "evidence-based faith" concerning the Good News, which is very different from gullibility or from blind faith. Nor is it something you can work yourself into.

Faith, or trustfulness, is the foundation of every form of relationship. You don't know how much to trust someone you've just met. It is only by experience with a person that trust and relationship are able to form and grow. This is true for every human relationship, and it is also true for getting to know God.

The epistle of Jude uses the word "faith" to describe the systematization of what the apostles believed and taught. His reference to "faith once and for all delivered to the saints" (Jude 3) implies a complete and discernible body of knowable facts, anchored in history and is the gospel message, the tradition of the Church.

The tradition of apostolic doctrine is a severe contrast to what is usually claimed in modern liberal seminaries—that Christian doctrine has evolved under the influence of culture. This liberal concept forms the basis of the Modernist theology that grew so prominently in the last century. However, what the apostles experienced and learned from Jesus is fixed in history. Those who want the Church to "get with it" regarding modern times can't change the past, and were they to succeed in promoting something new, in reality they would have created a new religion.

The Mechanism of Faith in Justification

In considering "justification by faith," what do we understand by "justification?" The Greek word for "just" is *dikaios*, which in English means righteous. Justification, then, is the means by which one becomes righteous in the sight of God.

Paul's words "the upright man finds life through faith" (Romans 1:17) are a quote from the prophet Habakkuk: "The upright man will live by his faithfulness" (Habakkuk 2:4). (Many readers may be more familiar with the KJV: "The just shall live by faith.") This could be taken two ways. It could mean that a righteous man lives a life of faith, or it could mean that an unrighteous man becomes righteous (justified) by his faith, that is, by what he believes. Luther embraced the second meaning so strongly as to coin the phrase "faith alone."

We have to be cautious not to oversimplify what we mean by faith and the mechanism by which it relates to justification. It has to be more than intellectual assent to facts, as James warned of demons believing "but trembling with fear."(James 2:19). The demons fully believe the facts but to no avail.

For the word *justification,* the dictionary offers a theological example: "Justification can be construed as a theological use of a legal term meaning that the sinner is declared to be righteous or justly free from the obligation to the penalty."[6] The Protestant Reformers, especially Calvin, understood justification in the terms of the law court. Calvin's picture of original sin was that fallen man was totally depraved. The underlying concept was that the punishment deserved by the sinner had been meted out on Jesus at the cross so that God's justice was satisfied. The sinner was then given a verdict of "not guilty" and his sin "covered" by the cross. But there is a real danger here, of making the concept of justification into a legal fiction. Did the now justified sinner actually change—become righteous—or was it only his legal status that was changed by the verdict? Such a concept of justification risks being like placing a different label on the bottle without changing its contents.

A liturgical example of Calvin's theology is demonstrated in the Anglican Litany, a service of prayerful supplication.[7] The people's response in the original Latin was "miserere nobis," or literally "have mercy on us." Under the influence of Calvin's teaching in the sixteenth century, reflecting the idea of total depravity and the law court concept, the new translation into English was, " have mercy upon us miserable sinners." It kept the poetic cadence of the Latin but changed the meaning. How can a person who is the temple of the Holy Spirit at the same time be a miserable sinner? Still totally depraved? Paul wrote to the Corinthians, "Your body . . . is the temple of the Holy Spirit, who is in you since you received him from God" (1 Corinthians 6:19). "You are God's chosen race, his saints" (Colossians 3:12).

Jesus taught that even sinners were capable of good actions. "For if you love those who love you, what right have you to claim any credit? Even tax collectors do as much, do they not?" (Matthew 5:47). If this be the case, these sinners could not have been totally depraved if they are capable of loving one another. Perhaps Calvin's philosophical presuppositions influenced him to overlook this, and similar verses, by selective reading of Scripture. After all, he did profess Sola Scriptura as his authority. No one is immune to oversight.

The Role of Faith in Justification

The creation story in Genesis tells of God interacting with Adam and Eve in the garden of Eden. This divine/human inter-relationship appears to have been intended as an integral part of creation, to be lived out in this world. But since the encounter with the serpent and the resulting fall, we have abandoned our role in that relationship by rebellion and pride, thereby becoming sinners.

In this situation we are unable to work our own way into becoming blameless before God. It was he who initiated the process for restoration of relationship by sending us his Son, whose cross and resurrection provided the means for our way back to him. This was God's grace, or gift, freely offered to us. Not our effort, but his gift. "It is through grace that you have been saved" (Ephesians 2:5). The whole purpose was the reestablishment of a living relationship with God, not simply "a ticket to heaven." Such an offer needs to be received to become effective. The foundation of faith is essential for us to be able to respond to the offer of God's grace and restore that original relationship with him. Without grace, our belief would be in vain. Without faith, or trusting him, we would be unable to receive the grace he offers. Both are involved in the achievement of justification, and this is also what the Catholic Church teaches.

Faith is the essential ingredient of every human relationship, and it is formed by an orderly process. First is the introduction that establishes acquaintance. Next is the encouragement that comes through the experience of taking little steps of trust. When we feel secure in these, we reach a degree of trust that enables us to interact and form a relationship or friendship.

Justification that establishes a relationship with God works in the same way. We have to be introduced to the facts about God and the plan of salvation. From this, acquaintance and the building of trust make interaction possible. Such trust is the faith that Paul talked about: "The just shall live by faith" (Romans 1:17). "For by grace you have been saved through faith" (Ephesians 2:8, RSV). This is the sort of trust that is able to receive the free gift of grace and then embark on the lifelong journey of interactive relationship with God and thereby live the Christian life.

The closeness of this relationship was expressed by Paul when he wrote to the church in Corinth that anyone who is "in Christ" is a "new creation" (2 Corinthians 5:17). It describes the transformation of the whole heart and soul. Jesus himself prayed, "Father, may they be one in us, as you are in me and I am in you" (John 17:21). This prayer expresses the supreme degree of intimacy expected in this relationship. It is the will of Jesus for the whole Church to be "in Christ."

Coming to Faith

The first Early Church record of anyone coming to faith as a result of evangelism was at the Jewish feast of Pentecost after the Holy Spirit had filled the apostles. By Peter's anointed preaching, the Holy Spirit stirred the hearts of a huge crowd who were then "cut to the heart" (Acts 2:37). These were Jews who had come to the festival and were already familiar with many of the facts about God. Not only did they believe what Peter said, but the Spirit deeply moved them and they asked, "What must we do?" Peter said, "You must repent . . . you must be baptized in the name of Jesus Christ for the forgiveness of your sins" (Acts 2:38).

"Repent and be baptized." This brings up another question: does baptism have a role in justification? In the Great Commission, Jesus said, "Go, therefore, make disciples of all the nations; baptize them in the name of the Father and of the Son and of the Holy Spirit" (Matthew 28:19). He also told Nicodemus, "Unless a man is born through water and the Spirit, he cannot enter the kingdom of God" (John 3:5). These words of Jesus imply that baptism is indeed a part of the equation. He went on to clarify this to Nicodemus: "You must be born from above" (John 3:7; the KJV says "again"). Baptism is not simply an order to be obeyed (an ordinance), but rather something that appears to be intended to impart grace "from above." Otherwise it would not have to be "from above."

Perhaps because of such stories in the New Testament depicting the response of adults to the gospel message followed by baptism, the Radical Reformers insisted on "believer's baptism" as the only biblical practice, and it is the normal pattern among evangelicals today. However, for the preceding fifteen centuries, the Catholic and Orthodox Church baptized infants with the intention that they might receive grace "from above" and become members of the body of Christ. At Philippi, Lydia responded to Paul's preaching, so "she and her household" were baptized (Acts 16:15). Later, the jailer in the same community responded "and was baptized then and there with all his household" (Acts 16:33). In both these instances, the households were likely to have included young children who were presumably baptized along with the rest of them. The absence of those details in Scripture does not preclude this probability.

Later, in the days of the Early Church, adults who wanted to become Christians were given in-depth instruction that lasted up to two years before they were baptized. During this time they were called "catechumens," and when attending the Eucharist, they were dismissed after the Scripture reading and sermon to go out for instruction. For infants of Christian parents, the lengthy instruction was deferred until long after their baptism.

The Life of Faith and Justification

When considering faith and justification, our theology is often caught in a philosophical warp. The Greek dualism underlying our cultural heritage denigrates the value of the physical world, with the common major thrust on "getting to heaven." Where does this emphasis put God's purpose in creating the physical world and its people? Six times in the creation story in Genesis we are told that God saw all he had created and that it was "good" or "very good." From this it should be evident that God valued the world and the people he created. Surely he values the lifetime we live on this earth which he has given us.

If God created man in his own image, it must have been for a purpose. When the fall of man occurred, it did not turn his love for us into hatred, nor did it cancel his purpose for creating us. He is the one who initiated the means of restoration: "For God sent his Son into the world not condemn the world, but so that through him the world might be saved" (John 3:17). This is not a picture of an angry God looking for faults to punish, but rather a Father desiring to pick up and rescue the ones he created and loves. It is a true gift of grace freely offered.

Crossing the Starting Line

The intention of justification is not that a one-time act of faith that will entitle an individual to a ticket to heaven. It's common for preachers to claim to have obtained a certain number of "salvations" as a response to their message. The Greek verb for "saved" is *sozo*, which in Scripture is used in the past, present, and future tense. The past tense refers to what Jesus did on the cross to procure our salvation. The present tense is what the preacher means by "getting saved," the response to the gospel message with the intent to follow Jesus. The future tense is for when we reach heaven. When a person "goes forward" in answering an altar call, that is not the totality of the meaning of salvation, but rather it is the stepping across the starting line of the conscious Christian walk, whether before or after baptism.

God's intention is the restoration of a living relationship with him while we are still in this physical world, and this relationship is not limited to isolated individuals but is established with us as the body of Christ. It is the nourishment of our Lord's relationship with this body that is the intention of the Eucharist in the Ancient Church. It is Jesus's prayer for the Church, as his body, to be one in him in a close, living relationship of faith. Heaven comes as a benefit of this relationship, which begins and has value during our life on this earth. It is this relationship which should be our focus.

Faith Alive

The faith involved with justification consists of fidelity that comes from the heart. The epistle of James says, "You see now that it is by doing something good, and not only by believing, that a man is justified" (James 2:24). He clarifies his meaning with the example, "A body dies if it is separated from the spirit, and in the same way faith is dead if it is separated from good deeds" (James 2:26). These works are manifestations of our faith. In other words, they are the results that flow from faith and which are essential for Christian living. Behavior is the product of fidelity because it flows from the heart.

Paul told Titus to "preach the behavior which goes with healthy doctrine" (Titus 2:1). Our behavior has to flow from our faith relationship. James just does not support "faith alone" but sees good works as part of the package. The relationship of faith is critical in our Christian walk, but so also is our behavior if our loyalty to Jesus is real. God desires to relate to the physical world and the people he created and enjoy their free choice to want to relate to him. For this relationship to be lived out on our part constitutes holiness.

God created us in his own image, and that included the ability to make choices. This ability not only allowed us to interact with God but also came with the possibility of our choosing to rebel; hence, we were able to fall. If God had made us unable to make choices and so be unable to fall, we would have been created as puppets instead of people made in his image, thus preventing the problem of evil. We may not fully understand why we were allowed the ability to choose; this limitation of understanding is probably "because our brain fits inside our head."[8]

Faith and grace have been the Church's expression of how justification is achieved from the very beginning. Love, grace, faith, baptism, and the life of the Church all are all intimately involved in the process, and all will leave a void if we try to separate them from it. True faith is multifaceted and is a God-enabled response to grace and fidelity for an interactive relationship with him. Works and behavior are intimately connected with it. Our goal is to continually walk with the Lord here and now, with heaven as a future benefit.

Understanding the means of justification is a most critical and basic area of the Christian faith. For all of us to have any hope of the unity desired by Jesus, it is urgent we understand just what we believe by it for ourselves, to communicate with other denominations as to what they understand by it, and then to communicate openly with each other instead of going by mistaken assumptions about what we think others believe. When we truly understand each other, we are finally in a position to pursue the unity Jesus prayed for.

CHAPTER 12

WHAT ABOUT THE KINGDOM?

What is our Lord's intention for the kingdom and its relationship to the Church? In his Great Commission (Matthew 28:19), Christ's ambitious intention is to bring into the fold people from every ethnic group on the planet. What is the purpose of doing so? It's not limited to sifting the world for candidates to populate heaven, which would imply that the physical world has no value or role for "kingdom living" on this earth. But Jesus taught his disciples to pray "thy kingdom come, thy will be done on earth as it is in heaven" (KJV). He must have cared about the nature and value of continuing life in this world.

Our Lord's focus was on the kingdom. A kingdom has to be united under its king. It is essentially a central authority of governing. The people Jesus came to save have their entry point to this kingdom via his Church in this world. If Jesus prayed for his body, the Church, to be one, we should do it his way willingly. If the entry is in this world, we should understand what "world" means.

It is all too common to understand the spiritual meaning of the word "world" in Scripture as referring to the physical world. Such a confused identification comes from the Gnostic philosophy of the first and second centuries that considered physical matter to be evil. We as Christians should have a problem agreeing with this. Unfortunately, our cultural heritage includes it, and this idea can still infect our theological thinking. When James wrote about "pure, unspoilt religion" including "keeping oneself uncontaminated by the world" (James 1:27), he was referring to avoiding contamination by the culture and philosophy of the pagan world around them. That is what Scripture means by "worldliness."

To view the physical world as being evil rejects God's assessment of creation. Jesus was born into this world as a real physical baby entering the material world. This should confirm the value of creation and the people created in God's image. From this we should conclude that our Lord has a definite purpose for his Church and kingdom to have a presence on this earth.

The Relationship of Church and Kingdom in the World

When reading through the gospels, we see that Jesus talked a great deal about the kingdom. *Young's Analytical Concordance*[1] gives 107 references for this topic. Luke tells us Jesus "made his way through towns and villages preaching and proclaiming the Good News of the kingdom of God" (Luke 8:1). The kingdom, the Church, and the gospel are intimately connected. The gospel of Mark declares the kingdom is "close at hand" with a need for repentance (Mark 1:15). It is also "like a tiny mustard seed that grows," (Mark 4:31), and it needs to be welcomed as a little child welcomes (Mark 10:15).

Jesus gave an intriguing agricultural example of the kingdom in the parable of the darnel, or "tares," where this wheat-like weed was sown in a field by an enemy. Both wheat and darnel are let grow to maturity lest some wheat be pulled in the attempt to remove the weeds earlier (Matthew 13:24–30). Explaining this to the apostles, Jesus identified the harvest as the end of the world where the angels gather "out of the kingdom" all who do evil, not separating them out prior to that.

This presupposes that the kingdom is already in the world and is made up of all sorts of people, good and bad, side by side. Peter's second letter clarifies the intent in this pattern: "The Lord is not being slow, but he is being patient with you all, wanting nobody to be lost and everybody brought to change his ways" (2 Peter 3:9). The Church, as the kingdom in the world, consists of real people—some saintly, many average, and some of only marginal spirituality. The Church as a community, by influence and encouragement, gives the opportunity for all to be converted and grow in relationship with God. Whether individuals respond or not is ultimately their own choice.

Membership

Mark said in his gospel that we must welcome the kingdom as a little child does. In John's gospel, Jesus told Nicodemus that to see the kingdom required being born from above, by water and the Spirit (John 3:3–5). This graphic picture of becoming a member of the kingdom was understood by the Ancient Church to represent Christian baptism, which we experience in this world. But we read in John that Jesus told Pilate his kingdom was not of this world (John 18:36). In other words, it is a heavenly kingdom, but entry into it and early experience of it is extended to the Church on earth. Although the kingdom is on earth, it does not belong to the earth. This kingdom has eternal dimensions since it was present at the time of the apostles and at the same time is yet to come even in our own day.

Just What Is a Kingdom?

In American culture, we don't give much thought to the meaning of kingdom. It has been well over two hundred years since we experienced life under a king. Freedom and self-determination have been our heritage. When we think of government models, we think of a democratic republic and elected representatives. Most denominations have adopted this pattern for the government of their churches. Cherishing the spirit of independence, one might be tempted to dream of a Republic of Heaven.

But a true kingdom is not a democracy. The ruler of the kingdom is not elected and has no term limits. God permanently rules. His subjects are not a collection of isolated individuals but rather a loyal and obedient people, an interconnected community, "a holy nation" (1 Peter 2:9, KJV).

The Church, as a people, involves all ethnicities, races, and nations. Their uniqueness lies in their relationship to Jesus and what he did on the cross. Peter wrote, "But you are a chosen race, a royal priesthood, a consecrated nation, a people set apart. Once you were not a people at all and now you are the people of God" (1 Peter 2:9–10). God works miraculous changes in the hearts of those who are "in Christ," and those connected to him are intended to become connected to one another as a people.

Independence and separation, whether by schism or by denominational stance, are not God's intention for Church. Paul reminds us: "So all of us, in union with Christ, form one body, and as parts of it we belong to each other" (Romans 12:5). *"All of us."* This indicates that all Christians in different parts of the world are intended to somehow be connected as parts that form the one worldwide body. In diversity, yes, but not independence. Here, the Church is pictured as being like a human body with Christ as the head. Just as all the parts of the human body are necessary for it to be complete and fully functional, so it is with the Church. To become disconnected from the body is to become disconnected from the head.

Jesus as head loves all the parts of his body. We expect that one part of the body ought to love and cherish the rest of the body members. If the Church is the body of Christ, then we, like Jesus, should love the Church. If we dislike, distrust, deny membership to a part of the body, our animosity is directed against a part of Christ. Looking back to the sixteenth and seventeenth centuries, we saw how Catholics and Protestants burned and killed each other to "stamp out error." For the same reason Protestants burned, drowned, and beheaded other Protestants. These activities were a flagrant dismemberment of the body of Christ. Certainly in this world, the body of Christ does have warts, and it does get sick, but Jesus doesn't want to dismantle it but rather to heal it. Warfare among body parts is more like cancer than obedience to the king.

Becoming a People of the Kingdom

When Jesus talked with Nicodemus about entry into the kingdom, he used the family metaphor of birth. For the classic Christian or Jewish family, birth does not occur in isolation. Here, a physical birth involves a mom and dad along with the concern of relatives and friends. The baby is born as an individual but is totally dependent on family to survive. Even before birth, the baby is anticipated by parents, aunts, uncles, siblings, and grandparents, who all expect to form a relationship with the new infant. In a sense, the baby is born as already a part of the community of family. It is not a revocable relationship. When you are family, you are stuck with your relatives. Values and traditions are absorbed as you grow up in the family. Your individuality is not lost by being part of a family, but a large part of your identity is connected to it. In a sense, growing up is "discipleship training" for life as part of that family.

Coming into the kingdom via the Church is similar. One is born individually into it in baptism, as it has been since the Church began. (The Ancient Church understood this baptism to initiate the individual's membership into the body of Christ, not only locally, but as a worldwide membership.) Like in a physical family, the individual is not alone as he is baptismally birthed into the Church. The Church body anticipates his birth "from above by water and the Spirit."

Inner conversion of the heart is an integral part of the life of the baptized Christian. In the New Testament accounts of adults being baptized, they respond to the gospel and then seek baptism. Evangelicals see this response as "getting saved," a prerequisite for baptism. The Catholic term for this response is "conversion." Catholics do require learning the faith and undergoing conversion. For those baptized in infancy, this response of faith develops over time while "growing up" in the Church and includes catechetical instruction. It is not less real.

The Ancient Church understanding of conversion goes beyond any one-time event. It is understood as a process that has a beginning and continues growing for a lifetime. The conscious part of the journey does begin with the decision to follow Jesus, but it does not end there. Conversion has a sense of an ongoing, daily re-committal and growth in the faith relationship. It is personal, but in the context of community and not in an unbiblical individualism consisting of "just me and Jesus" in a purely private manner that would make the Church superfluous. John tells us that on the night of his betrayal, Jesus prayed for the apostles, and "I pray not only for these, but for those also who through their words will believe in me" (John 17:20). He was also praying for us and all who have come to know him as a result of the apostles' ministry. He continued,

"May they all be one. Father, may they be one in us as you are in me and I am in you, so that the world may believe it was you who sent me." We are to be a united kingdom. Internal strife promotes disintegration. If one part of the human body is at odds with another part, the body's functioning is crippled—it is "a house divided against itself"(Mark 3:25). This also holds true for the wholeness of the Church.

Mission of Disintegration

We should not be surprised to find that forces of disintegration are working to undermine the unity Jesus prayed for. In fact, we should *expect* this, given that the earthly part of the kingdom is constituted of fallible human beings. If you were the devil, how would you plot to destroy the Church? Perhaps the most useful ploy would be to plant distrust of authority. It would be much easier to make the Church question fallible human leaders that it was to tempt Eve to question the integrity of God!

The Protestant Reformers were convinced they had achieved a great victory by throwing off what they considered to be the oppressive authority of the Catholic Church. However, their choices came at a cost. Unintentionally, they were in effect driving a wedge into the earthly kingdom. The elimination of apostolic succession in the ministry disrupted the historic connection to the apostles, and along with the rejection of tradition, this in effect removed the authority of authenticated history and doctrine. It opened the possibility for the new ideas of the Renaissance worldview to influence the doctrines replacing them.

It took a great deal of courage for the Reformers to separate themselves from the security of the Church that had raised them. This move had to be justified in their minds in order for them to have any peace about it. It is not surprising, then, that they so strongly vilified the Catholic Church, not only on charges of moral corruption but also with accusations of inventing "nonbiblical" doctrines and practices. Immorality among Church leaders in the early sixteenth century was undeniable and did require attention. The charge of inventing doctrines and practices was another matter. The use of liturgy and Eucharistic doctrine, along with episcopacy, was already well established long before 155 AD—little more than two generations after Jesus lived on earth. Renaissance humanism encouraged the Reformers to disestablish those longstanding apostolic traditions. In all fairness, we must recognize that it's almost certain the Reformers did not have access to much of the historical documentation concerning that early tradition that has now become easily available as the result of technology. Back then every book and document had to be copied by hand, and therefore literature was available at limited locations. Even so, knowingly or not, they cast off much that had been part of the Church from its ancient beginning.

Suspicion and bitterness grew over the intervening centuries. In 1746, a couple of centuries into the Reformation, George Whitefield, the outstanding preacher of the Great Awakening in America, received news of the defeat of Bonnie Prince Charlie at Culloden. Had he not been defeated, Charles would have become king of England, and he was Catholic. Whitefield responded to the news by preaching "a sermon of thanksgiving to God" for saving England and the colonies from becoming subjects of a Catholic monarch. Whitefield is reported to have said that if that had happened, "How soon would our pulpits everywhere have been filled with these old anti-Christian doctrines, free will, meriting by works, transubstantiation, purgatory . . . and all the other abominations of the whore of Babylon?"[2]

Even to the present day, such vitriolic sentiments are nourished by significant numbers of Protestants, continuing the great divide in the global Church. Thankfully, the animosity has softened slightly since the 1960s. The response to Vatican II (which required translation of the liturgy into the language of the different peoples around the world), the Charismatic Renewal, and the election of a Catholic president (JFK) are evidence of this. And the softening is definitely a two-way street. Pope John XXIII made overtures to ecumenism even prior to calling Vatican II and by having Catholic representatives as observers at the World Council of Churches in 1960.[3] Subsequently, commissions have been set up by the Catholic Church to engage in discussion with various Orthodox, Anglican, Lutheran, and other major Protestant groups. This work continues to the present and is not a matter of doctrinal compromise, but rather of opening a conversation to increase understanding. It is a Catholic contribution to the pursuit of true unity.

The Charismatic Renewal effected grass-roots conversation and increased understanding among the many denominations involved. Our political climate today is increasingly hostile to Christian values, and our response has encouraged interdenominational cooperation to protect common areas of the faith. Evangelicals and Catholics are finding that they have many critical values and beliefs in common. Among these are the concern about abortion clinics, marriage and family, and the immorality that is supported and sponsored by education and government. Points of contact have resulted from taking joint action in these matters that have encouraged discussing our faith across the lines.

Who Is Who?

On some level, in fact, this closing of the gaps is dramatic. When we talk about evangelicals and Catholics acting in cooperation, we might wonder just who is included in which category. Mark Noll, in *Evangelicals and Catholics Together,* summarized a number of diverse denominations that can be categorized as evangelicals in America. Based on a survey of religion and politics in America, he found that "evangelicals" include thirteen varieties of Baptists, six of Pentecostals, eight of Holiness groups, five kinds of Lutherans, and several kinds of Methodists and Congregationalists as well as many independent and nondenominational churches.[4] Noll also referred to a Canadian study, reported in *Maclean's Magazine,* that 15 percent of Canadians consider themselves evangelicals. The real surprise is that among these, one third of them were practicing Roman Catholics.[5] This begins to blur the lines of distinction at the popular level. People are willing to talk, work cooperatively, and pray across denominational lines. In this, we can see real signs of progress and hope.

Even so, division remains, and it remains ugly. If we are to bridge the waters, we must remember that when our own church teaches us what another denomination believes, we can't assume it is unbiased and free from conflict of interest. To accurately understand what another denomination believes requires patient, prayerful dialogue with active, committed members of such a community. There are real and significant differences between us, but we need to keep them in perspective. What a word or term means to one denomination may mean something quite different in another.

Keep in mind that in the human body, not all the parts look alike. This is because they all have a different function that is critical for the rest of the body. In the same way, we should expect the body of Christ to have some diversity, but this should never become a division that cuts a part off. In our sin, over the centuries we have experienced the attempt to cut off parts with the claim that they are not real Christians. By whose authority do we support such amputation?

When Jesus gave his agricultural example of the kingdom concerning the wheat and the darnel, he pointed out that the darnel is not removed until the harvest, lest some wheat be uprooted. The Church, as the earthly entry to the kingdom, has the task of aiding all members to come alive in the faith. Our duty is not to pull up weeds but to encourage all the wheat. This is our calling. We need to love the Church as Jesus does if we are to be obedient to his will. To live and share the gospel, we have to be kingdom minded and not purveyors of denominational political correctness.

CHAPTER 13

HOPE FROM THE PRIMITIVE CHURCH

Despite the progress we do see in our day, the deeply divided Christian Church can be a source of grief and even despair to anyone who takes Jesus's prayer in John 17 seriously. But we may find hope by turning to the Early Church—not because they were pure, simple, or pristine, but because they were a lot like us.

In John's Revelation, Jesus gave John a message for each of the seven local congregations in what is now Turkey. They were not pictured as seven independent churches, but as seven local manifestations of "the Church" (Revelation 1:1–3:22). Jesus told John to write to "the angel" of each one with a message. "The angel" could not have been an angel in heaven, because Jesus could simply speak to one without John's help. The Greek word for *angel* means "messenger," and it is used here as a symbolic term to denote the bishop. John was to communicate the message to the bishop in each of the seven cities. As *episkopos*, the bishop was the authoritative messenger of the gospel for his city.

A unique message was given to the congregation of each city to deal with their need. Ephesus was becoming deficient in love. Smyrna was about to face trials and needed encouragement. Pergamum was facing false teachers and was too lax in keeping the faith, even allowing Nicolaitans to have some influence among them. Thyatira had a "Jezebel prophetess spirit' and laxity of faith. Sardis was moribund and in urgent need of revival; Philadelphia needed to "hang on."

The mysterious Nicolaitans were reported by the Early Church historian Eusebius as being a briefly popular subculture who in the attempt to "subdue the flesh" tried to "treat it with contempt."[1] They were influenced by the Greek dualistic philosophy where the spirit was good and the physical was essentially evil. Since only the spirit mattered, these people considered fleshly activities to be disconnected from it. Because of this, they ended up allowing promiscuity. Nicolaitans were rejected in Ephesus but tolerated in Pergamum, perhaps because they were considered to be "spiritually minded."

The seventh church, Laodicea, was accused of being lukewarm. It saw itself as what we in our day might consider the pinnacle of success. Perhaps it was somewhat like a successful modern megachurch. It had financial independence and seemed to meet everyone's needs. There was no complaint of moral scandal or of heretical teaching. It would appear to be an example to emulate. Yet the message for them was "you are neither cold nor hot . . . I will spit you out of my mouth" (Revelation 3:16). The Greek term gives the sense of vomiting.

The True Early Church

Each of the seven churches of John's vision was a true early New Testament congregation. They were only a few decades old at that time. They had the benefit of teaching by the apostles themselves and were in apostolic fellowship with the rest of the Church. Even Sunday worship was most likely similar to what is described in Acts 2:42 and would have consisted of "breaking of bread" and "the prayers." Yet, in spite of having all these benefits, they had significant problems and were at risk of serious consequences.

Five of these churches had problems needing correction and were called upon to repent. Ephesus was told that if they did not repent and change, their lampstand (their local congregation) would be removed. Pergamum was told to repent or suffer divine retribution. Thyatira was told that unless they repented, children would suffer. Sardis had to repent and wake up or face the consequences of being moribund. Laodicea had to repent "in real earnest," after which Jesus would stand at the door and knock. Notice that none of these churches had to change doctrine, nor alter their practice of worship, nor mess with their authority structure. They had slipped in their focus and their behavior. Not one of these congregations was to be abandoned, nor replaced if they repented and regained their proper focus and behavior.

Hope for Us Today

As unsettling as these vignettes may be, they should give us hope for the Church in our own day. These early Christians were not perfect people any more than we are, but they all had some genuine degree of commitment to our Lord. Amazingly, God was still able to use them mightily. In less than three hundred years this imperfect Church, with "real-life" Christians, evangelized the territory around the Mediterranean, and the empire as a whole became Christian. The gospel even spread as far as India. God does do miracles with those who are committed and available, even within a flawed Church. In the parable of the wheat and tares, Jesus indicated the tares would not be removed out of the kingdom until final judgment. Why should we expect him to do otherwise now, or in the sixteenth century?

God did not start with perfect people, but with those who would listen. In Genesis, Abraham listened as God promised that all the tribes of the earth would be blessed through him (Genesis 12:3). There is frequent mention in the Old Testament of God's reaching out to the nations, especially in Isaiah and Jeremiah. At the potter's shed, God showed Jeremiah how he desired to be interactive with his people. God would even "change his mind" according to how they responded (Jeremiah 18:6–10). This Jewish picture of God would be totally unacceptable to Greek philosophical attributes of deity, which precluded any possible "divine changing of mind," yet such an ability to change a response is essential for an interactive relationship.

After the people of Judah were disciplined by going to Babylon, God had Jeremiah encourage them. "I know the plans I have for you . . . plans for peace, not disaster, reserving a future full of hope for you. Then you will call to me, and come and plead with me. I will listen to you . . . When you seek me with all your heart; I will let you find me" (Jeremiah 29:11–14). Wholeness of heart is the key.

Scripture clearly shows that God is not an angry despot ready to destroy people or condemn them to hell, despite some theological opinions to the contrary. Rather, we see in the gospel of John that he so loved the people in the world that he sent his Son to die, not to condemn but to save (John 3:16–17). Paul reminds us that to be "in Christ" is to become a new creation (2 Corinthians 5:17). The whole desire of the heart of God is for his people to be interactive with him with their whole heart.

The Call to Be Church

We have emphasized that the call to "be Church" was a call to "be a people," specifically the people of God. The New

Testament Church in Jerusalem was such a community of people. It was organized and had an authority structure, and it was more than likely united in worship (Acts 2:42). Above and beyond this, Jesus had charged the apostles to make disciples of all the nations. And this they did despite having imperfections.

Presently, we not only have flaws such as we saw in the Early Church, but we now have the added burden of the multidenominational disarray to complicate our efforts. The spirit of independence impairs attempts to work together to further the kingdom. Without unity or communication, the natural tendency is to drift apart.

Drifting and Safeguards

In his epistle, Jude wrote, "Fight hard for the faith which has been once and for all entrusted to the saints" (Jude 3). "Once and for all" indicates the complete faith was in place with no intention for it to drift or evolve. The epistle to the Hebrews also warns the Church to "turn our minds more attentively than before to what we have been taught, so that we do not drift away" (Hebrews 2:1). Both these Scriptures urge the Church to fastidiously maintain the doctrine and tradition of Jesus and the life of the Church

The sacraments, especially the prominence of the Eucharist in the pre-Reformation Church, helped resist drift. Receiving the Lord's body regularly nourished the intimacy of the relationship with Jesus for both the individual and the whole community that participated. This made them sort of blood brothers and sisters in the Lord, strengthening their oneness.

The creeds, we remember, came into existence within the first three hundred years of the Church, before the New

Testament was assembled. These safeguarded the key points of doctrine from apostolic times onward about God, the plan of salvation, and the life to come. They were eventually incorporated into the liturgy as a weekly reminder of the basics of the faith, and they continue in use today.

It is unfortunate that such early expressions of faith are so often neglected in modern churches today. My wife and I were in a prayer meeting of young missionary students when the leader asked if anyone knew the Apostles Creed. We looked about and realized we were the only ones in the room who did. It is sad because the knowledge of the contents of the Apostles Creed and the Nicene Creed do offer some hope toward unity of all Christians to be on the same page in articulating the faith as it was known near the beginning of the Church.

In many denominations since the Reformation, these particular safeguards have become less familiar. Changes to tradition, authority, and sacrament have removed or revised old anchor points. Like the agricultural parable of tares, in response to "sin in the house," the Reformers uprooted wheat of significant safeguards as well as weeds of immoral behavior. The result was a simpler Christianity, but now deprived of good and helpful areas of the faith and strength for the journey.

It would be helpful to revisit the situation at the time these changes were made, to assess the degree of wisdom involved in making them. We need to re-examine Scripture and pray over these areas, and then with calm and cool heads discern what was truly of God's direction and what was at least partially inspired by the Renaissance humanist milieu of the day.

What Now?

Should a miracle occur and all the lost anchor points and safeguards be restored, and we became one as Jesus prayed for, would we then be much different from the five churches in John's vision in Revelation who needed to repent? There is no unique "right way" in the New Testament Church, nor in the pre-Reformation Church, that would make us into the ideal Church. The essential key is how the Church interacts with its Lord.

"So repent in real earnest. Look, I am standing at the door, knocking" (Revelation 3:19–20). This is the plea to wake up, change, and return to interaction with Jesus. "If one of you hears me calling and opens the door, I will come in to share his meal, side by side with him" (Revelation 3:20). Jesus is ready to receive us back from the brink. It is not a forceful coercion, but it requires us to be willing to respond, not only as individuals, but as the corporate Church body.

Our Lord has provided means of grace within the Church for two millennia to assist us in our walk with him. He wants us as a whole community, as the whole body of Christ, to walk with him. His gifts of grace are to assist us on the journey. To ignore or reject these means of grace is to say "no thanks" to the gifts he offers us. If they would be helpful to walking with the Lord, shouldn't those in Protestant denominations consider the possibility of revisiting them? It would require becoming familiar with these gifts, to decide on how much to accept. But to simply persist with a spirit of independence is giving in to our sense of pride.

To begin the journey to the oneness Jesus prayed for, we need a firm foundation. God offers means of grace to us as gifts of love because of the love he has for his whole Church as well as for us as individuals. Grace is not to bless us so we can continue in sinful living but to effect a genuine change. We are not supposed to be miserable sinners with a legal judgment of "not guilty"; rather, by our experience with him we are actually to become holy. This involves effort on our part—a choice, a decision. "Make a habit of obedience: be holy in all you do . . . be holy, for I am holy" (1 Peter 1:14–16 as a quote from Leviticus 19:2). A whole Church community actively seeking the face of God, opening the door to Jesus as he knocks, transforms the whole life and atmosphere of the Church and the lives of individuals. This is the fruit of repentance. This is what the New Testament Church in Revelation was supposed to do.

And this is the call to the whole Church today. It is the only way that the fractures can be healed and pride let go. Such a turn can't be legislated, like the laws enforcing "correct belief" and the resulting atrocities of the sixteenth and seventeenth centuries. Laws promote loopholes. It is only by what is in the heart, that true holiness is possible. The fruit of the Spirit is what we should seek as our response to the cross. Love, joy, peace, patience, kindness, goodness, faithfulness, gentleness and self-control are the picture of the maturing walk of faith, not by force of coercion, but from the heart (Galatians 5:22).

All the Christians in the world make up the body of Christ, and we need to be aware that the body exists and that we are part of it. The New Testament makes frequent references to the analogy of the human body. It is significant for getting our brain around Jesus' prayer for oneness. We have to care about the whole body beyond the tiny part of it that we belong to. The parts of a human body are connected, but more importantly, they communicate with each other. To stub a toe or burn a finger communicates and galvanizes the whole body into action.

We as the body of Christ need to re-establish communication and so "learn each other's language" and what we mean by our unique features and concerns. Full obedience requires being connected. If we focus on our own vision alone, we miss seeing the big picture. The shattered body needs healing to restore healthy connections and coordination. How is that possible? If the churches in Revelation did it, why can't we?

CHAPTER 14

SOLUTION IMPOSSIBLE?

We began this journey by looking at Jesus' prayer for his followers to be one. Unfortunately, our Lord's urgency for this oneness is not taken seriously by most Christians today, as evidenced by the hundreds or even thousands of separate denominations in the world. But the New Testament repeatedly advocates the importance of the unity as being analogous to the human body. Many Christians claim that instead of a divided Church, we have "diversity" to account for the variety of denominations. It is sort of like a menu—you choose the variety that most meets your needs. In a sense, "diversity" is being used as if it were a form of unity. But the existence of prejudice and animosity among denominations and against the Ancient Church belies the seriousness of true division.

It is urgent that we realize that no matter which brand of Church we attend, whether Protestant or Catholic, there is really only one gospel message, only one plan of salvation, and only one New Testament. Why then is it so important to maintain thousands of independent denominations to express this one faith? The tragedy is accepting division but calling it "diversity."

Just What Is Diversity?

What do we mean by *diversity, division,* and *reconciliation*? Because of the complexity of human nature, there will always be diversity. Rightly understood, this does not preclude unity. The dictionary lists the meaning of *diversity* as "distinctiveness, being opposed to identity."[1] It is not disunity but rather being "not identical."

A good illustration is the family. Each member is an individual. Each one has a distinctive personality, looks, physique, gifting, and interests. All members of a family are individuals, but they are not independent of each other. There is a sense of belonging and a bond of love. Those in the family are an "us," and those outside are a "them." The connection to one another is permanent, with loyalty, interdependence, and a bond of heart. Family members are diverse individuals, not identical, but not independent.

Church diversity should look like family, where variations of expression are possible without the need to disassociate from the rest of the Church. For instance, the diversity in the Orthodox Church tends to be along ethnic lines, but this whole Church has the same threefold ministry, doctrines, and sacraments. It is sort of like siblings in a family. The Anglican Church is similar to this. The umbrella of the Catholic Church also includes ethnic diversities such as the Uniat churches (like Greek Catholic or Ukrainian Catholic), but they are connected to the one Catholic Church around the globe.

All Christians should be able to fit into a 'diversity' without the need to be in separation from the rest of the Church. There has to be a path for those who have separated themselves from the Ancient Church to migrate from division into diversity. Maintaining the basics of the gospel message and the inerrancy of Scripture will help reduce the gap of separation. Reconnection of separated body parts may be humanly impossible, but with God all things are possible. We need to seek his plan instead of eagerly protecting our own turf.

Diversity and Division

Division has a more sinister meaning than does diversity. The dictionary describes *division* as "to cut or separate into parts . . . to cause to separate; disunite; break up; keep apart."[2] Division is the diametric opposite of unity. Even in the metaphor of family, division can occur through quarreling, which, without reconciliation, may erupt into a feud dividing that family. This is the sort of thing that has happened to the Church, both in 1054 in the East/West Schism and again in the sixteenth century, and such quarreling and division continues to happen to the present day.

The Protestant Reformation marked the beginning of the great multiplication of independent denominations. These separations resulted in not only division and disunity, but also in enmity and competition for converts. The staggering increase in the number of independent denominations and their doctrinal differences makes it obvious that the Reformers, in their enthusiasm to make changes, had inadvertently discarded valuable parts of the faith that had previously kept the Church unified. The lack of an agreed standard of interpretation across the denominations is probably the most serious culprit for division.

Tradition in a single church is a powerful stimulus for its own unity. Where multiple churches are in competition and have incompatible traditions, these differences create potent forces for division. Most Protestants officially eschew tradition, but after five hundred years since the Reformation, nearly all denominations still generally adhere to the doctrine and interpretations of faith and Scripture that were taught by their founders. These "denominational traditions" can be incompatible with those of different denominations, for example, infant baptism vs. believers baptism, sprinkling vs. total immersion, predestination vs. free will. At communion, Lutherans accept the Real Presence of Jesus in the bread and wine, but generally Protestants insist the body and blood of Jesus are purely metaphoric. Naturally we think we are the ones with the truth, and it is the others who are in error. In reality, unless we are willing to face the possibility of being fallible, we could be more directed by "religious political correctness" than we are by the truth.

To pursue the oneness Jesus prayed for, we have to start from where we are. We need the openness to hear what others mean by what they believe even if we've been taught otherwise. Our focus has to be on the Lord and not on our need to be right. Information won't hurt us, but it may open the door to communication and willingness to pray together. It would be the genuine start of a process of growing into scriptural unity as in John's gospel. Understanding, communication, and prayer are the critical ingredients.

If, as Barrett claims, there are now over thirty-seven thousand Protestant denominations,[3] the issue may not be as severe as it looks. The Christian faith is not so complex as to support that many discrete theologies. Surely we should expect to see families of denominations that are quite similar to each other, and indeed, it's possible a few are essentially identical.

Jesus used the picture of the relationship within the Trinity when he prayed for the unity he desires for his Church. The interrelationship of the Trinity is devoid of independence, yet, Father, Son, and Holy Spirit are not identical. As in the human body all parts are necessary—eye, ear, foot, finger—so it is in the Church. Each congregation is unique, with its own area of gifts, evangelism, urban mission, youth work, etc., and like a finger or eye, it is to be connected to the rest of the body. Each congregation (or denomination) should likewise be a part of the community of the whole Church and connected to the head, rather than cherishing independence. The parts of the Church are not intended to be identical but rather to be complementary and to act with love toward each other.

Reconciliation?

The dictionary defines *reconcile* as "restore friendship, reunite alienated friendship, adjust the differences." In view of the gross differences of doctrinal stance among the huge array of denominations today, we might wonder if there is any hope that reconciliation is possible—not only between individuals but corporately for the body. Over the last century there have been efforts toward unity in the Ecumenical Movement. This word comes from the Greek *oikos,* which means "house." (The original British spelling was *oecumenical,* but in the American usage, the "o" was dropped.) The sense here is for the whole Church to be "under one roof." Various degrees of the movement have sporadically arisen and had some influence. A few interdenominational efforts have had impact at improving relationships as well. The Billy Graham Crusades used interchurch cooperation to good effect. Interdenominational mission organizations have come also into being on the basis of cooperation, but laudable as that may be there is still little progression toward a true unity of the body.

We have previously noted that the East/West Schism of 1054 was declared healed by the Council of Lyons in 1274, but this was never implemented. Pope John Paul II dreamed of participating in that Orthodox/Catholic reunion and being able to have a joint Eucharist, concelebrated by both East and West, in time to welcome the new millennium. If that had happened, more than five-eighths of the world's Christians would have been reconciled by the union or reconnection of fellow "body parts."

Corporate Merger?

Yet, even if the denominations of the world were to experience a corporate-style merger to achieve unity, considerable compromise of both doctrine and tradition would be required, which would not address the areas of faith that are in dispute. On a small scale, this has been attempted for a few Churches possessing compatible doctrine, such as the union of Methodist, Presbyterian, and Congregational Churches in Canada in 1925 to form the United Church of Canada. (Not all congregations of the component denominations joined this union.) The Church of South India was a later result of a similar unification. To attempt to do this on a larger scale, it would be critical to address all the areas in dispute, especially since five hundred years of Protestant traditions could pose extreme complications and offer no protection from drifting. Without resolving the disputed areas, any such effort is doomed to failure.

For the whole Church to come to oneness in this sense, it would likely require that every Christian on earth hear the audible voice of God commanding it. Barring this eventuality, we can certainly hope that a lesser goal may be within reach as a starting point toward true unity, such as appreciating what needs to be understood within each of the areas in dispute. For this to happen, it will require us to be involved in friendships on a large scale where true, deep discussion is possible.

Seven of these areas we have previously examined are:

- The Creeds
- Sola Fide
- Sola Scriptura

- Apostolic Succession with Authority and Tradition
- The Ancient Sacraments
- Liturgy
- The Meaning of "Oneness" in Church Unity

The denominational dogmas concerning these areas are capable of producing a response ranging from mild dispute to apoplexy. Dare we hope for unity with our wide range of perceived "absolute truth"?

With all the variety of competing Protestant churches, you might wonder what the Catholic Church thinks about Protestant churches in general. If you expect condemnation, you may be in for a surprise.

Under the title "Wounds to Unity," the Catechism of the Catholic Church states:

> **Paragraph # 817:** In fact, "in this one and only Church of God from its very beginnings there arose certain rifts, which the Apostle strongly censures as damnable. But in subsequent centuries much more serious dissentions appeared and large communities became separated from full communion with the Catholic Church—for which often enough, men from both sides were to blame."

> **# 818:** "However, one cannot charge with the sin of separation those who at present are born into these communities . . . and in them are brought up in the faith of Christ, and the Catholic Church accepts them with respect and affection as brothers . . . All who have been justified by faith, in Baptism are incorporated into Christ; therefore have the right to be called Christians, and with good reason are

accepted as brothers of the Lord by the children of the Catholic Church."

And most, surprisingly we read next:

> **# 819:** "Furthermore, many elements of sanctification and of truth" are found outside the visible confines of the Catholic Church: "The written Word of God; the life of grace; faith, hope, and charity, with the other interior gifts of the Holy Spirit, as well as visible elements." Christ's Spirit uses these Churches and ecclesial communities as means of salvation, whose power derives from the fullness of grace and the truth that Christ has entrusted to the Catholic Church. All these blessings come from Christ and lead to him, and are in themselves calls to "Catholic unity."

We can see from these statements that the Catholic Church recognizes Protestant churches as having legitimate effectiveness; in spite of the fact that the Reformers had rejected multiple key areas of the Catholic faith, God still uses them. Could Protestants have the same grace toward other Protestants or toward the Catholic Church? Whether we are Catholic or Protestant, holding to the complete apostolic tradition or an incomplete one, God uses those who are willingly available.

Solution Possible?

Before any discussion about the possibility of resolving the division amongst Christians, the Church must agree that instead of simple diversity, true disunity is the major reality. Unfortunately, there will always be dissenters who insist they are the only true

Christians and the rest of us need to join them to be saved. At the opposite extreme are those so liberal as to deny any supernatural realities, such as miracles, the virgin birth of Jesus, his deity, resurrection, and ascension, and the efficacy of the cross.

The extremes of the spectrum will never be interested in exploring any resolution of divisions. However, the majority of those between these extremes already hold the most basic core Christian doctrines, including the divine inspiration of the Bible. Among these lies the hope of pursuing true reconciliation and full obedience to Jesus.

The core doctrines form solid anchor points in the movement toward unity, but other doctrines in the divided Church must also be considered. We've previously seen that though we may share the core beliefs, they are more like a table of contents rather than the whole DNA of the unity Jesus envisioned. Had this core been sufficient, such divisions would never have occurred. It is the Renaissance worldview with its spirit of independence that has given permission to rupture those DNA strands of original unity. Therefore, it behooves us to reexamine our own worldview and its implications for our doctrines in light of history.

Finding a Path to Obedience and Reconciliation

Any attempt by our own particular church to be reconciled with every individual one of the hundreds of denominations out there would be an impossible task. It would make more sense for each church to trace its own ancestry back to where true unity did exist in order to understand how we got to where we are. We need to discover the roots from which we grew without despising them. Where were the serious mistakes made along that journey? Are we prepared to be "politically incorrect" if that is where the evidence leads?

Few Christians know many details of their own denomination's origins, but we need to understand that lineage if we are to gain a proper perspective. If we could identify each point of division along the way, and patiently examine the divisive issues, it could open the way toward true oneness. Looking at these issues, we might be surprised to find that our churches have held to the same or similar meanings, but by using different words, they produced division. We may be amazed at how much secular philosophy influenced the choices made at the time of parting of the ways compared to the scant role played by the Jewish and early Christian worldview.

Fully unraveling the roots of your particular denomination might require more academic competence than you possess, but you don't have to be a scholar to act with charity toward denominations with viewpoints different from your own. We do have to know what we believe and why, but this does not prevent us from asking people of other denominations what they believe and what they understand by it. Their answers need to be taken as "information to mull over" rather than something to argue about. Reciprocity in this area could increase the possibility for clearing up misunderstanding and offer help to heal conflict. This would constitute a true early stage of reconciliation.

To have any hope of being part of the solution instead of part of the problem, we need our own house to be in order. We need to understand our own faith, take it seriously, and seek to develop an intimate, committed, heart relationship with Jesus. Paul expressed this relationship as being "in Christ" (2 Corinthians 5:17). Though it may begin with the intellect, it must become a reality of genuine heart and passion, with humility and sincerity. This means going well beyond the first step of crossing the starting line ("getting saved") and into the lifelong journey of a growing relationship with our Lord, as he intended for every Christian. It means "walking the walk."

Further, putting our house in order requires repentance and forgiveness. The majority of our denominational forbears were all guilty of advocating the use of force to condemn error as they interpreted it. Churchmen of succeeding generations forged ahead with their own ideas to enforce "correct doctrine." Gross atrocities were committed against fellow Christians who held different opinions in order to "stamp out error." All that was accomplished was the deepening of division.

The outcome of those efforts was a virtual defiance of Jesus's intent, a gross disobedience. To disobey God is sin, as was the arrogance and pride that accompanied that disobedience. If our corporate past actions causing division and our present toleration of it are to be forgiven, we need a repentance such as that recorded in Daniel 9. This prophet urgently, on behalf of all the people, repented of the sins of the nation that had put them into captivity in Babylon. Our churches today need to jointly repent in earnest for the sins that have produced the divisions we have today. We must repent for excusing the violence used in the past to enforce "unity," and we must repent for accepting division and calling it diversity. We must repent collectively for speaking against other denominations, usually on the basis of unsubstantiated information, no matter how "good the authority" that was its source.

After having repented, we then need to offer, and ask for, forgiveness of the other denominations for our complicity in tolerating division. This must be corporate and across denominational dividing lines. When Peter asked Jesus how many times he needed to forgive, Jesus said seventy-seven times (sometimes translated as seventy times seven; Matthew 18:21–22). It always has to begin with an act of will, and the heart will follow later. Wounds to the body of Christ have festered far too long, allowing the enemy to make deep inroads into our territory.

Our highest priority has to be to pray. We must together seek God across all the dividing lines to ask for his leading for how we should proceed. We pray, not to get God to bless our own plan for unity, but for us to listen and hear his voice.

It is true that some denominational doctrine may preclude our hearing. But I hope that a personal story about planning a mission outreach may be encouraging in this regard.

Our mission team was requested to each pray separately for a week and then meet and share what each had received from the Lord. Some had a picture of brown-skinned people, not black or white. Several had pictured unusual yellow flowers; another, an airport. I had an "angle" and trees without tops; another had a grass house on stilts. The angle fit Sumatra, but the leader could not get a response from contacts there. Nevertheless, our focus turned to that area of the world. The outcome was to go to the Philippines.

We did a medical outreach on a large island where there had been a typhoon that had done much damage and torn the tops off many palm trees. The people were brown-skinned. My wife and I stayed overnight in a grass hut on short stilts. On return from this medical portion of the trip, our team was housed in Baguio City in a YWAM base beside the airport. The runway was surrounded by the unusual yellow flowers. If God can give such leading on a short-term mission trip, can he— and will he—not give leadership through our prayers for the reconciliation of the whole Church?

Praying, talking with other Christians, and soaking our thinking in Scripture are all within the capability of each one of us. Likewise, we are capable of taking a fresh look at history, of asking ourselves difficult questions, and of getting honest about where we come from. We might find it profitable as well to revisit some of the means of grace discarded by the Reformers, especially as we realize the influence of humanism on their actions. We must come to fully understand the difference between diversity within the body and division of the body.

We face a world that is increasingly anti-Christian and a culture that encourages a multiculturalism that is more accommodating to other religions. With the growth of ISIS and militant Islam, the secular humanist political correctness of the media and what is being taught in our public schools, the influence of the ACLU, and increasing government mandates that encroach upon areas of conscience, now more than ever Christians urgently need to speak out with one united voice. If we accept being divided and conquered, truly we are ignoring the Great Commission to our peril.

The easy interdenominational interaction during the Renewal movement in the 1960s, '70s, and early '80s points a way forward: it would be valuable to again socialize with Christians of other denominations who also believe the Bible to be true and inspired by God. Evangelicals are not the only ones who believe this way. It might go against the way you have been taught, but Catholics and Orthodox were, from the beginning of the Church, the original believers in God's plan of salvation and the efficacy of the cross. They are also Bible-believing Christians who believe in the need for faith, personal relationship with Jesus, and continual growth in that faith relationship. They consider that the sacraments offer means of grace to aid and strengthen our walk with the Lord, which is to continue as a lifelong relationship and grow in intimacy. In fact, to recover their full understanding might help us replant the wheat that came out by "pulling the tares" during the Reformation.

It's not by experts nor by democratic vote but by a genuine revival that the difference can be made for true oneness. All Christians need to focus our hearts on Jesus, not so our own plan for unity will be blessed, but to full-heartedly seek and be obedient to his plan. With us as humans, the goal is unreachable, but with him, remember, all things are possible. We must seek God's help for us, as Christians of diverse traditions, to become friends and communicate and seek his plan and then run with it. To be truly reconciled we have to be willing to be part of the whole body of Christ and not just our own small corner.

Do we have the courage to face the challenge of obeying the will of Jesus concerning unity for his Church, or will we yield to political correctness? To be fully committed to Jesus is to be committed to his body, the whole Church, and to the unity for which he prayed. Never forget that the heart of God is for an interactive personal relationship with each of us and with the Church as a whole body at the same time.

> Do all you can to preserve the unity of the Spirit by the peace that binds you together. There is one Body, one Spirit, just as you were all called into one and the same hope when you were called. There is one Lord, one faith, one baptism, and one God who is Father of all, over all, through all and within all.
>
> (Ephesians 4:3–5)

NOTES

Chapter 1

1. Personally offered by Scott Tompkins, YWAM Woodcrest School of Writing, Lindale, TX. 2013.

2. Bob Franke personally related this incident, used here with his permission.

3. David Barrett, George Kupion, Todd Johnson, *World Christian Encyclopedia,* vol 1. (New York: Oxford Press, 2001), vii.

4. Ibid, 18.

5. Ibid, 16.

6. Ibid, vii.

7. Ibid, 4; fig. 1-1.

8. Ibid, 4; fig. 1-1.

Chapter 2

1. Charles Swindoll, *The Church Awakening* (New York: FaithWords, 2010), 14.

2. Ergun and Emir Caner, *Unveiling Islam* (Grand Rapid, MI: Kregel Publications, 2002), 204.

3. Francis Frangipane, *It's Time to End Church Splits* (Cedar Rapids, IA: Arrow Publications, 2002), i.

4. Ibid, 5.

5. Ibid, 9.

6. E. Glenn Wagner, *The Awesome Power of Shared Beliefs* (Dallas: Word Publishing, 1995), 10.

7. Ibid, 37–38.

8. Ibid, 37–38.

Chapter 3

1. Eusebius, *The Church History*, trans. by Paul Maier (Grand Rapids, MI: Kregel Publications, 1999), 110.

2. Kenneth Scott Latourette, *A History of Christianity* (New York: Harper & Bros., 1953), 116.

3. Ibid, 117.

4. Ibid, 130.

5. Eusebius, *The Church History*, trans. by Paul Maier (Grand Rapids, MI: Kregel Publications, 1999), 111.

6. Ibid, 146.

7. Kenneth Scott Latourette, *A History of Christianity* (New York: Harper & Bros., 1953), 131.

8. Ibid, 123.

9. Ibid, 124.

10. Ibid, 125.

11. Ibid, 127.

12. Eusebius, *The Church History*, trans. by Paul Maier (Grand Rapids, MI: Kregel Publications, 1999), 181.

13. Kenneth Scott Latourette, *A History of Christianity* (New York: Harper & Bros., 1953), 135.

14. Kenneth Scott Latourette, *A History of Christianity* (New York: Harper & Bros., 1953), 197.

15. Ibid, 200.

16. Ibid, 90.

17. Ibid, 91.

18. Ibid, 92.

19. Iris Habib Masri, *The Story of the Copts* (Jasper, AR: End Time Handmaidens, 1982), 98.

20. Ibid, 100.

21. Ibid, 100.

22. Ibid, 101.

23. Ibid, 104.

24. Ibid, 104–105.

25. Kenneth Scott Latourette, *A History of Christianity* (New York: Harper & Bros., 1953), 15.

26. *The Works of Philo,* trans. by C.D. Yonge (Peabody, MA: Hendrickson Publishers, 1995), 393–394.

27. *The Works of Josephus,* trans. by William Whiston (Peabody, MA: Hendrickson Publishers, 1987), 311–312.

28. Eusebius, *The Church History,* trans. by Paul Maier (Grand Rapids, MI: Kregel Publications, 1999), 115.

29. Kenneth Scott Latourette, *A History of Christianity* (New York: Harper & Bros., 1953), 134. See also "367 Athanasius Defines the New Testament—Famous Festal Letter," *ChristianityToday.com,* http://www.christianity-today.com/ch/1990/issue 28/2812.html.

30. "Third Council of Carthage (A.D. 397)," *Bible-Researcher. com,* http://www.bible-researcher.com/carthage.html.

31. Kenneth Scott Latourette, *A History of Christianity* (New York: Harper & Bros., 1953), 232.

Chapter 4

1. W.K. Ferguson and Geoffrey Brunn, *A Survey of European Civilization* (Cambridge, MA: Houghton Mifflin, 1952), 119.

2. C.W. Previte-Orton, *The Shorter Cambridge Medieval History*, Vol. 1 (London: Cambridge University Press, 1952), 119.

3. W.K. Ferguson and Geoffrey Brunn, *A Survey of European Civilization* (Cambridge, MA: Houghton Mifflin, 1952), 132.

4. C.W. Previte-Orton, *The Shorter Cambridge Medieval History*, Vol. 1 (London: Cambridge University Press, 1952), 130.

5. Ibid, 163.

6. W.K. Ferguson and Geoffrey Brunn, *A Survey of European Civilization* (Cambridge, MA: Houghton Mifflin, 1952), 143.

7. C.W. Previte-Orton, *The Shorter Cambridge Medieval History*, Vol. 1 (London: Cambridge University Press, 1952), 194.

8. Ibid, 194.

9. Philip Freeman, *St. Patrick of Ireland* (New York: Simon & Schuster, 2004), 68.

10. Ibid, 70–71.

11. James Hitchcock, *A History of the Catholic Church* (San Francisco: Ignatius Press, 2012), 105.

12. Kenneth Scott Latourette, *A History of Christianity* (New York: Harper & Bros., 1953), 133.

13. James Hitchcock, *A History of the Catholic Church* (San Francisco: Ignatius Press, 2012), 106.

14. Ibid, 107.

15. Kenneth Scott Latourette, *A History of Christianity* (New York: Harper & Bros., 1953), 337–338.

16. W.K. Ferguson and Geoffrey Brunn, *A Survey of European Civilization* (Cambridge, MA: Houghton Mifflin, 1952), 168.

17. Kenneth Scott Latourette, *A History of Christianity* (New York: Harper & Bros., 1953), 339–340.

18. Ibid, 273.

19. W.K. Ferguson and Geoffrey Brunn, *A Survey of European Civilization* (Cambridge, MA: Houghton Mifflin, 1952), 170; and C.W. Previte-Orton, *The Shorter Cambridge Medieval History*, Vol. 1 (London: Cambridge University Press, 1952), 159.

20. C.W. Previte-Orton, *The Shorter Cambridge Medieval History*, Vol. 1 (London: Cambridge University Press, 1952), 295.

21. W.K. Ferguson and Geoffrey Brunn, *A Survey of European Civilization* (Cambridge, MA: Houghton Mifflin, 1952), 171.

22. Kenneth Scott Latourette, *A History of Christianity* (New York: Harper & Bros., 1953), 329.

23. W.K. Ferguson and Geoffrey Brunn, *A Survey of European Civilization* (Cambridge, MA: Houghton Mifflin, 1952), 177.

24. Ibid, 186.

25. Ibid, 217.

26. Ibid, 218.

27. Kenneth Scott Latourette, *A History of Christianity* (New York: Harper & Bros., 1953), 573.

28. Ibid, 575.

29. C.W. Previte-Orton, *The Shorter Cambridge Medieval History*, Vol. 1 (London: Cambridge University Press, 1952), 519.

30. Ibid, 519.

31. Kenneth Scott Latourette, *A History of Christianity* (New York: Harper & Bros., 1953), 410.

32. C.W. Previte-Orton, *The Shorter Cambridge Medieval History*, Vol. 1 (London: Cambridge University Press, 1952), 521.

33. Kenneth Scott Latourette, *A History of Christianity* (New York: Harper & Bros., 1953), 411.

34. Ibid, 411.

35. Ibid, 411.

36. Ibid, 412.

37. Ibid, 625.

38. Ibid, 627.

39. C.W. Previte-Orton, *The Shorter Cambridge Medieval History*, Vol. 1 (London: Cambridge University Press, 1952), 596.

40. Kenneth Scott Latourette, *A History of Christianity* (New York: Harper & Bros., 1953), 630.

41. Ibid, 628.

42. C.W. Previte-Orton, *The Shorter Cambridge Medieval History*, Vol. 1 (London: Cambridge University Press, 1952), 616.

43. Ibid, 620.

44. Ibid, 620.

45. Ibid, 620.

46. Kenneth Scott Latourette, *A History of Christianity* (New York: Harper & Bros., 1953), 604.

47. C.W. Previte-Orton, *The Shorter Cambridge Medieval History*, Vol. 1 (London: Cambridge University Press, 1952), 630.

48. Ibid, 630.

49. Ibid, 630.

50. Kenneth Scott Latourette, *A History of Christianity* (New York: Harper & Bros., 1953), 636.

51. Ibid, 636.

52. Ibid, 636.

53. Ibid, 637.

54. Ibid, 637.

55. Ibid, 637.

56. Ibid, 638.

57. Ibid, 639.

Chapter 5

1. Karl Adams, *Roots of the Reformation* (Zanesville, OH: CHR Resources, 2012), 57.

2. *College Standard Dictionary* (New York: Funk & Wagnalls, 1946), 98.

3. C.W. Previte-Orton, *The Shorter Cambridge Medieval History*, Vol. 1 (London: Cambridge University Press, 1952), 661.

4. Kenneth Scott Latourette, *A History of Christianity* (New York: Harper & Bros., 1953), 430.

5. Cardinal Joseph Ratzinger, "The Primacy of the successor of Peter in the mystery of the Church," Symposium report, Dec. 1996, www.ewtn.com/library/curia/cdfprima.htm.

6. Kenneth Scott Latourette, *A History of Christianity* (New York: Harper & Bros., 1953), 118.

7. Jordan Ballor, "Luther and The Epistle of Straw," article in *The Calvinist International*, June 2013, https://calvinistinternational.com./2013/06/13/luther-and-the-epistle-of-straw.

Chapter 6

1. Charles Swindoll, *The Church Awakening* (New York: FaithWords, 2010), 15.

2. *Catechism of the Catholic Church* (New York: Doubleday, 1995), Paragraph # 1558.

3. Ibid, Paragraph #1562.

4. Kenneth Scott Latourette, *A History of Christianity* (New York: Harper & Bros., 1953), 528.

5. *The Book of Common Prayer* (Toronto: Anglican Book Centre, 1959), 550.

6. *Catechism of the Catholic Church* (New York: Doubleday, 1995), Paragraph #774.

7. Kenneth Scott Latourette, *A History of Christianity* (New York: Harper & Bros., 1953), 200.

8. *Catechism of the Catholic Church* (New York: Doubleday, 1995), Paragraph #1302.

9. Ibid, Paragraph #1617.

10. Ibid, Paragraph #1447.

11. *New St Joseph Sunday Missal* (Totowa, NJ: Catholic Book Publishing, 2015), 18–19.

12. Prof. Andrew C. Fix, *The Renaissance, the Reformation and the Rise of Nations* (Chantilly, VA: Great Courses, The Teaching Co., 2005). Audio.

Chapter 7

1. Kenneth Scott Latourette, *A History of Christianity* (New York: Harper & Bros., 1953), 662–663.

2. Ibid, 656.

3. Henry Lucas, *The Renaissance and the Reformation* (New York: Harper & Bros., 1934), 626.

4. Kenneth Scott Latourette, *A History of Christianity* (New York: Harper & Bros., 1953), 657.

5. Ibid, 658.

6. Henry Lucas, *The Renaissance and the Reformation* (New York: Harper & Bros., 1934), 305.

7. Kenneth Scott Latourette, *A History of Christianity* (New York: Harper & Bros., 1953), 846.

8. Ibid, 855.

9. Ibid, 672–673.

10. Ibid, 673.

11. Henry Lucas, *The Renaissance and the Reformation* (New York: Harper & Bros., 1934), 290.

12. Kenneth Scott Latourette, *A History of Christianity* (New York: Harper & Bros., 1953), 673.

13. Ibid, 843.

14. Ibid, 847.

15. Henry Lucas, *The Renaissance and the Reformation* (New York: Harper & Bros., 1934), 643.

16. Ibid, 643.

17. Ibid, 650.

18. Kenneth Scott Latourette, *A History of Christianity* (New York: Harper & Bros., 1953), 866.

19. Henry Lucas, *The Renaissance and the Reformation* (New York: Harper & Bros., 1934), 653.

20. Ibid, 656.

21. Kenneth Scott Latourette, *A History of Christianity* (New York: Harper & Bros., 1953), 847.

22. Ibid, 869.

23. Ibid, 840.

Chapter 8

1. Kenneth Scott Latourette, *A History of Christianity* (New York: Harper & Bros., 1953), 698.

2. Ibid, 701.

3. Ibid, 605.

4. Henry Lucas, *The Renaissance and the Reformation* (New York: Harper & Bros., 1934), 419.

5. Kenneth Scott Latourette, *A History of Christianity* (New York: Harper & Bros., 1953), 704.

6. Ibid, 705.

7. Henry Lucas, *The Renaissance and the Reformation* (New York: Harper & Bros., 1934), 430.

8. Kenneth Scott Latourette, *A History of Christianity* (New York: Harper & Bros., 1953), 706.

9. Henry Lucas, *The Renaissance and the Reformation* (New York: Harper & Bros., 1934), 431.

10. James Hitchcock, *A History of the Catholic Church* (San Francisco: Ignatius Press, 2012), 256.

11. Henry Lucas, *The Renaissance and the Reformation* (New York: Harper & Bros., 1934), 434.

12. Kenneth Scott Latourette, *A History of Christianity* (New York: Harper & Bros., 1953), 708.

13. Ibid, 708.

14. Ibid, 710.

15. Ibid, 708.

16. Ibid, 711.

17. Ibid, 713.

18. Ibid, 713.

19. Ibid, 716.

20. Ibid, 720.

21. Ibid, 722.

22. Henry Lucas, *The Renaissance and the Reformation* (New York: Harper & Bros., 1934), 508.

23. Ibid, 508.

24. Ibid, 512.

25. Ibid, 513.

26. Ibid, 516; and Kenneth Scott Latourette, *A History of Christianity* (New York: Harper & Bros., 1953), 726.

27. Henry Lucas, *The Renaissance and the Reformation* (New York: Harper & Bros., 1934), 517.

28. Kenneth Scott Latourette, *A History of Christianity* (New York: Harper & Bros., 1953), 751–752.

29. Henry Lucas, *The Renaissance and the Reformation* (New York: Harper & Bros., 1934), 571–572.

30. Ibid, 580.

31. Kenneth Scott Latourette, *A History of Christianity* (New York: Harper & Bros., 1953), 755.

32. Henry Lucas, *The Renaissance and the Reformation* (New York: Harper & Bros., 1934), 581.

33. Ibid, 583.

34. Ibid, 585.

35. Ibid, 578.

36. Ibid, 613.

37. Kenneth Scott Latourette, *A History of Christianity* (New York: Harper & Bros., 1953), 770.

38. Ibid, 771.

39. Arthur Herman, *How the Scots Invented the Modern World* (New York: 3 Rivers Press, 2001), 2–6.

40. Kenneth Scott Latourette, *A History of Christianity* (New York: Harper & Bros., 1953), 799.

41. Ibid, 811.

Chapter 9

1. Kenneth Scott Latourette, *A History of Christianity* (New York: Harper & Bros., 1953), 780.

2. Henry Lucas, *The Renaissance and the Reformation* (New York: Harper & Bros., 1934), 522.

3. J. Gordon Melton, *Nelson's Guide to Denominations* (Nashville: Thomas Nelson, 2007), 222.

4. Kenneth Scott Latourette, *A History of Christianity* (New York: Harper & Bros., 1953), 781.

5. Henry Lucas, *The Renaissance and the Reformation* (New York: Harper & Bros., 1934), 523.

6. Ibid, 526.

7. Ibid, 522.

8. Ibid, 522.

9. Ibid, 524.

10. Kenneth Scott Latourette, *A History of Christianity* (New York: Harper & Bros., 1953), 784–785.

11. Ibid, 784–785.

12. Ibid, 784–785.

13. Henry Lucas, *The Renaissance and the Reformation* (New York: Harper & Bros., 1934), 525.

14. Kenneth Scott Latourette, *A History of Christianity* (New York: Harper & Bros., 1953), 786.

15. J. Gordon Melton, *Nelson's Guide to Denominations* (Nashville: Thomas Nelson, 2007), 289.

16. Ibid, 290.

17. Ibid, 291.

18. Ibid, 291.

19. Ibid, 291.

20. Ibid, 292.

21. Ibid, 299.

22. Ibid, 424–425.

23. Ibid, 424–425.

24. Ibid, 428.

25. Ibid, 429.

26. Ibid, 407.

27. Ibid, 410.

Chapter 10

1. C.W. Previte-Orton, *The Shorter Cambridge Medieval History*, Vol. 1 (London: Cambridge University Press, 1952), 661.

2. Ibid, 949.

3. Ibid, 949.

4. Kenneth Scott Latourette, *A History of Christianity* (New York: Harper & Bros., 1953), 664.

5. *Catechism of the Catholic Church* (New York: Doubleday, 1995), Paragraph #105–106.

6. Samuel Bagster & Sons, *The Analytical Greek Lexicon* (London: Samuel Bagster, 1925), 98.

7. Emily Belz, "The Battle for Accurate Translations," *World Magazine*, 2/25/2012, 44.

8. Kenneth Scott Latourette, *A History of Christianity* (New York: Harper & Bros., 1953), 179.

9. Samuel Bagster & Sons, *The Analytical Greek Lexicon* (London: Samuel Bagster, 1925), 125.

10. Exodus 28:30, Leviticus 8:8, Numbers 27:21.

11. Kenneth Scott Latourette, *A History of Christianity* (New York: Harper & Bros., 1953), 200.

12. Ibid, 200.

Chapter 11

1. Paul Little, *Know Why You Believe* (Downers Grove, IL: IVCF Press, 1968), 1.

2. Craig Keener, professor at Palmer Theological Seminary, Eastern University, Wynwood, PA, quoted in *Charisma Magazine*, 8/2010.

3. Kenneth Scott Latourette, *A History of Christianity* (New York: Harper & Bros., 1953), 1141.

4. Richard Dawkins, *The God Delusion* (New York: Houghton Mifflin, 2006), 199.

5. Kenneth Scott Latourette, *A History of Christianity* (New York: Harper & Bros., 1953), 127.

6. *College Standard Dictionary* (New York: Funk & Wagnalls, 1946), 629.

7. Anglican Church of Canada, *The Book of Common Prayer*, 1918 Revision, 39.

8. An expression frequently used by Larry Allen, teaching at School of the Bible, Tyler, TX.

Chapter 12

1. Robert Young, *Young's Analytical Concordance of the Bible*, 22nd edition (New York: Funk & Wagnalls, 1936), 573–574.

2. Mark Noll, *The History of an Encounter: Roman Catholics and Protestant Evangelicals*, Chapter 3, editors Charles Colson and Richard J Neuhaus, *Evangelicals and Catholics Together* (Dallas: Word Publishing, 1995), 90.

3. Ibid, 94.

4. Ibid, 104.

5. Quoted in ibid from George Rawlyk, in Angus Reid survey, "God is Alive: Canada is a Nation of Believers," special report in *Maclean's Magazine* (April 12, 1993), 32–50.

Chapter 13

1. Eusebius, *The Church History*, trans. by Paul Maier (Grand Rapids, MI: Kregel Publications, 1999), 118.

Chapter 14

1. *College Standard Dictionary* (New York: Funk & Wagnalls, 1946), 343.

2. Ibid, 343.

3. David Barrett, George Kupion, Todd Johnson, *World Christian Encyclopedia,* vol 1. (New York: Oxford Press, 2001), 18.